Pillars of Wealth, Book II

Finance and Business Essentials for Medical Practices

Yuval Bar-Or, PhD

TLB Publishing
Ellicott City, Maryland
www.TLBcorp.com

Copyright 2014 by Yuval Bar-Or

Cover photo: Barbara Glaeser

Cover by: Creative Jestures

Library of Congress Control Number: 2014932365

Library of Congress Cataloging-in-Publication Data

Bar-Or, Yuval, 1967-

Pillars of Wealth: Finance and Business Essentials for Medical Practices / Yuval Bar-Or

p.   cm.

ISBN: 978-0-9800118-4-5

1. Dental practice management 2. Medical practice management 3. Business and economics 4. Financial literacy 5. Risk management
I. Title.

TLB Publishing's books are available at wholesale discounts to educational institutions, corporations, and non-profits. For information, please contact us at: inquiries@tlbcorp.com.

Disclaimers: The information contained herein is provided for informational purposes only. It should not be construed as professional legal, financial or accounting advice. The content consists of general information which may not reflect current legal, accounting, or financial developments, verdicts or settlements, and most importantly, it is not specific to your particular circumstances. Any information contained herein is not intended to be a substitute for legal counsel or for advice from a licensed accountant or financial advisor. No one should act or refrain from acting on the basis of any content found herein but should instead seek the appropriate professional legal accounting and/or financial advice based on particular facts and circumstances. The author expressly disclaims all liability in respect to actions taken or not taken based on any of the contents of this book.

Acknowledgements

The *Pillars of Wealth* book series would not have been possible if not for the willingness of many busy professionals to share their experiences and advice. I thank Cynthia Mullen, MD, Ken Lewis, Charles Feitel, Jeanne Sanders, Nathan Crowe, Wayne Zell, Jeffrey Hausfeld, MD, Gareth Petsch, Don McDaniel, David Kovel, Dan D'Orazio, Christopher DeMarco, Ph.D., Andrew Giddens, Allen Schiff, Michael Limsky, Tracy Shen, Barry Rosen, Abba Poliakoff, Aaron Horne, MD, Sammy Zakaria, MD, Rani Hasan, MD, Ben Bashiri, Kirk Siegwarth, Thomas Sessa, Gai Cole, Rajiv Mahajan, Samuel Luxenburg, Michaela Muffoletto, David Leichter, Jeffrey Ring, Sanford Fisher, Michael Simmons, Erick Hosaka, DDS, Roger Samek, Felix Liao, DDS, Taylor Shoffner, Melissa Elliott, DDS, Xian Zoey Gao, Brett Weiss, Mark Rapson, Melissa Pitchford, Penny Doherty, Kathy Maddock, Ben Gorton, Andrew F. Howard, and Manuel Peregrino, MD.

Special thanks to Dipan Desai, MD, for his shared vision of delivering financial literacy education to medical professionals.

Failure to plan is planning to fail

— Benjamin Franklin

Table of Contents

Foreword

In the rapidly evolving healthcare marketplace, all physicians, new and established, employed and independent, will appreciate the thorough and detailed exam which Dr. Bar-Or gives to that most private and sensitive of areas—their personal and business finances.

Dr. Bar-Or follows up on his easy to read prescription for personal finances in volume one, with a careful dissection of how to organize, launch, run, grow, and protect a healthcare practice in volume two. His blueprint is a timeless algorithm that busy physicians should master early, and review often, just as they would with any classic of medical literature.

A medical practitioner can serve his patients best when his practice is on a sound financial and structural footing, with Dr. Bar-Or's latest consultation serving as both the foundation and the well-marked road map for long-term success.

Richard E. Rubin, MD, FACC
Bethesda, Maryland

Introduction

What This Book is About

This is the second book in the *Pillars of Wealth* series. Its objective is to provide practical and nuanced advice medical practitioners can use to make better financial and business decisions for their medical practices. The first book in the series, *Personal Finance Essentials for Medical Professionals*, focuses on helping medical professionals to make better financial decisions for themselves and their families.

The *Pillars of Wealth* book series addresses the general challenge that most doctors complete residency or fellowship without sufficient knowledge of business and finance. This educational deficiency often leads them to make sub-optimal decisions and leaves them vulnerable to potentially unqualified or unscrupulous salespeople pitching a variety of financial and business consulting solutions. More succinctly, the book series aims to help you level the playing field.

As explained in Book I, *Pillars* are the various assets we must strive to accumulate over our working lifetimes. These pillars or repositories of wealth support our family's financial wellbeing including our own dignified retirement. Pursuing multiple pillars is the logical risk management response to a world beset by economic, legal, and tax uncertainties. While any one pillar could be severely undermined by any of these factors, having wealth saved in other pillars provides much needed diversification and risk mitigation.

One of the pillars discussed in Book I is the financial value of a private practice and its general role as one of several potential pillars of wealth (others include real estate assets, investment accounts containing stocks and bonds, life insurance cash value, annuities, pension plans, etc.). While Book I surveys all the pillars, this book focuses entirely on exploring the aforementioned private practice pillar.

While this book stands on its own, I recommend you read both books in the series. The reason is that professional and personal financial decisions are intimately connected: when the medical practice is running smoothly, the success extends to personal finances. Similarly, when the private practice performs poorly, there is often an immediate and negative effect on the owner's personal finances. Some negative effects include the need to take shorter vacations or cancel them altogether, put off some desired purchases or home improvements, re-think expensive private college plans for children, etc. The connection is clearest in the most extreme cases, where the medical practice fails, as this can lead to financial devastation at a personal level. Causality can also run in the opposite direction. A poorly managed household can put strains on a business, and severe personal events including divorce can cause a medical practice to collapse.

There are many books addressing the management of private medical practices. Some focus on billing and coding, others on HIPAA and privacy issues, and yet others address any number of highly relevant topics. Quite simply, no single book can provide all the answers to every possible question about running a medical business. This book summarizes many of the major issues in an effort to give you a sense of the magnitude of the overall challenge of launching and running a medical practice. It primarily deals with three key topics, which include financial decision making, risk management, and human resource management. The book strives to provide multiple perspectives, through interviews with accountants, attorneys, health care business administrators, nurses, architects, real estate developers, real estate agents, marketing professionals, technical support and information technology personnel, etc., all of whom specialize in the medical services area. In this book, you are getting far more than the doctors' perspective.

Anecdotally, bankruptcy attorneys have reported higher bankruptcy rates for medical practitioners in recent years, and expect that trend to continue. This should not be a surprise to those of you already in private practice. You know that while payments from insurers have steadily decreased, staff wages have increased, as have the costs of meeting ever greater regulatory hurdles, as well as the costs of constantly evolving technological solutions. All of this combines to make it ever harder for medical practices to remain profitable. In order to survive and thrive, medical professionals must gain a solid understanding of finance and risk and make good decisions regarding the hiring and retention of the best employees.

On many occasions, I've spoken with doctors who feel they've already successfully addressed business planning issues and don't feel there is a need to discuss them. Often, they have a trusted financial advisor, accountant or attorney who helps them make decisions. In fairness, if they have indeed properly taken care of the issues, they shouldn't need to spend time on doing this again. But, in most cases I find that doctors *think* all issues have been addressed, when in reality they have not.

Insisting that an issue has been taken care of, and refusing to re-examine it, can mean depriving yourself of potential improvements. In the same way that a patient may benefit from a second opinion, you may benefit from asking: *have I really got things under control? Am I achieving maximum efficiencies? Do I need to take a fresh look at my business finances? Am I successfully and efficiently attracting the best staff members?*

A key observation when it comes to financial and human resource decision making is that the benefits of good decisions compound over a long time horizon. It follows that making poor decisions (and even just slightly suboptimal ones) and allowing them to fester severely undermines your financial health. It's far more effective to make better decisions early on than having to make up for lost time later.

I've attempted to minimize the use of jargon, instead seeking to use plain English. In some cases, I've used the professional economic, accounting or finance terminology, defining those terms directly in the text.

What motivated me to write this book series?

I'm a financial risk management expert. In some sense, I'm a physician for corporations and household finances. It's my duty to keep them healthy and functional. I also come from a medical family: my father and brother are both physicians, and there are several physicians and dentists in my extended family.

Prior to publication, the working title of this book series was "Sitting Ducks." This was a reflection of the feeling among many doctors that they are helpless, and constantly being targeted by financial services providers. To a great extent, these books are my response to the anxiety and helplessness felt by friends and family members in the medical community. My hope is that the content of this book series will help you understand relevant issues and take appropriate actions to protect your family and business.

Who This Book is For

This book is directed primarily at physicians and dentists in private practice, but is also highly relevant for pharmacists, chiropractors, alternative health care professionals, and veterinarians. For brevity I will use *doctor* to refer to all readers, although where the distinctions are relevant, I specify the medical profession.

Doctors who are interested in private practice need to be concerned with gaining business and financial decision making skills, but they are often consumed by the following priorities:

1. Providing high quality care
2. Getting desired medical outcomes
3. Keeping patient waiting-times low
4. Avoiding lawsuits
5. Spending time with family

The unavoidable reality, of course, is that without business and financial decision making skills, none of these high priorities are consistently attainable in private practice.

With the health care world growing more complex, more specialized, and more competitive by the day, business and finance savvy are necessary for survival. Inefficiencies must be identified and ironed out early on. Otherwise, they drag business performance down, and may ultimately pull a potentially viable business into bankruptcy.

If you wish to get a good start on a medical business, or to improve an existing one, then this book is for you.

The Private Practice Pillar

Book I began with a listing of three fundamental axioms for personal financial decision making. We begin this book with three fundamental competencies required for private medical practice success:

1. Be technically competent, or know your medical craft (as a dentist, physician, veterinarian, pharmacist, chiropractor, or alternative medicine healer)
2. Be technically competent as a business manager (understand the basics of accounting, finance, marketing)
3. Be emotionally competent (understand how to constructively deal with the people around you, including your staff and patients)

Most likely, you have the technical skills to fulfill the first competency. This book strives to enhance competencies 2 and 3.

Because so many new skills are needed when you own your own business, it's recommended that you don't jump immediately into private practice. Instead, it's better first to work for someone else for at least a year or two (ideally as an employee, but alternatively as an independent contractor). This provides an opportunity to refine your medical craft and pick up important business awareness and skills—*before committing significant time and money.*

Usually, you'll face a four-way fork in the road after a couple of years:

(1) Start your own practice
(2) Buy into your existing employer's practice
(3) Join another practice as an owner
(4) Go elsewhere as a junior staff member.

If you choose option 1, you should begin planning at least a year in advance of opening the doors for business. It can be wise to gradually reduce work hours at an existing place of work and steadily increase hours in your own new practice. This allows you to ease out of being an employee and into being an independent business owner. The alternative is to quit one job and begin the new practice from scratch, without enough clients or business experience to make ends meet—a precarious and inadvisable situation.

If you choose options 2 or 3, the path should be simpler because all of the prep work should have already taken place, including creation of all necessary infrastructure and hiring and training of staff. If the practice has been severely mismanaged, however, you may still have to go through all the practice building steps (outlined next) to clean house and move forward. In any case, it's advisable that you acquaint yourself with the history of the practice as this will explain to you why certain people feel a sense of ownership and may be upset in the event you attempt to change things.

If you find yourself gravitating to option 4, it may be that some part of you doesn't want to go into private practice. There's nothing wrong with that. It's good to figure that out sooner rather than later as you can avoid spending time and money unnecessarily.

The business of medicine has changed dramatically in just a few decades. Penny Doherty, front office manager at Signature OB/GYN in Columbia, Maryland, reminisces: "I still remember the good old days [Annapolis in the 1970s] when a waterman could trade some rockfish or premium oysters for a hernia operation."

Well, those days of casual barter are long gone.

Going into private practice means becoming a 21st Century business person, with all the burdens that entails. Yes, you are still a physician or dentist or chiropractor or veterinarian who wants to deliver medical services to those who need them, but you are embarking on a business venture. You may dislike marketing and accounting and finance, etc., but you must get used to those functions quickly. Either you will have to undertake them yourself, or you'll have to pay someone else to handle them, and when you hire others and rely on them, you need to be able to assess their performance and make tough decisions regarding their ongoing employment.

I interviewed dozens of professionals for this book (physicians, dentists, accountants, attorneys, health care consultants, medical practice administrators, real estate brokers, architects, contractors, etc.). While these discussions led to many useful observations, the most common was the observation that physicians and dentists are very smart people. The next most common observation was that physicians and dentists are often not very good business people. This is not meant as an insult. It is merely a reflection of the fact that doctors spend all their time on medicine, and next to zero time on learning business and finance basics.

On average, a young dentist tends to have more business knowledge than a young physician. This is largely attributable to the fact that the vast majority of dentists are destined for private practice and many dental programs provide some practice management education. Nevertheless, young dentists and dental school administrators are quick to point out that the business skills taught are relatively few and far between.

Recent graduates are almost always naïve regarding the complexity of starting a practice from scratch. They often have an overly simplistic expectation that they just need to find a good location, hire a nurse and receptionist, get some billing software in place and hang out their shingle—followed almost immediately by a rush of grateful patients and healthy revenue.

This book aims to give you a more accurate sense of the complexities of creating a new business or buying and running an existing practice. Given the complex business, legal, accounting and economic considerations, this book alone cannot make you an expert. Rather, the intention is to help you understand what you don't know, empowering you to form a solid team of experts who can help you realize your vision for a productive practice.

The idea of relying on others can be an uncomfortable notion for physicians, who are often trained to be self-sufficient decision makers. The key to a successful practice is to set up an environment in which you do what you are good at—seeing and treating patients—while your co-workers do what they are good at—freeing you up to see patients.

Emotional Intelligence & Competence

When you cross the line from an academic hospital setting to running a business you must acquire new skill sets. The obvious ones are the core concepts delivered by MBA courses on marketing, accounting, finance, etc. These are technical skills, in much the same way that surgery is a technical skill. The basics of these skills are covered in this book. None of these fall under the category of rocket science. That is, every reader easily has the intellectual capacity to learn and implement these technical skills.

Arguably, the more important workplace skills you must learn as an owner of a practice are the softer, people skills. These skills encompass constructive interactions with your patients. But they also must include constructive relations with your fellow staff members. It's easy to dismiss the importance of soft skills when dealing with staff. Many owners respond automatically with: *why should I spend time and energy on managing my staff? They're being paid to do a job, and they should just get on with it and leave their insecurities and personal dramas at home.*

It turns out that this attitude doesn't work well in a competitive human resources environment. Your best staff members can easily find a job elsewhere. The last thing you want to do is to encourage them to leave. Instead, you want to encourage them to stay, and to be most effective you need to have emotional competence, which begins with emotional intelligence.

Traditional or *Cognitive* (intellectual) capacity pertains to the mental processes of perception, memory, judgment, and reasoning. These are summarized by the traditional IQ measurement.

Emotional Intelligence is the capacity for self-awareness, motivation, self-regulation, empathy, and adeptness in relationships. In order to distinguish it from IQ, Emotional Intelligence is often referred to as EQ.

Cognitive skills (IQ) and emotional skills (EQ) are synergistic. Competence—the combination of traits, habits, and expertise that sets high achievers apart from less stellar performers—requires mastery of both cognitive and emotional capacities.

The key message here is that emotional intelligence is as critical to professional and personal success as is technical medical skill. The higher you rise in business, the more critical emotional competencies become. Consider a quote in Daniel Goleman's seminal book, *Emotional Intelligence: Why It Can Matter More Than IQ*. The quote is attributed to a head of research at a global executive search firm: "CEOs are hired for their intellect and business expertise—and fired for a lack of emotional intelligence."

As the owner of your small practice, you are most likely the CEO or equivalent. While there may not be anyone above you to fire you, the effect will be the same if you run the business into the ground and are forced to shut down operations.

Awareness of how emotions affect performance is the primary emotional competence: our emotions affect us, and the people around us; their emotions affect them, and the people around them (including us).

In order to move your medical practice forward, it's absolutely necessary for you to be emotionally competent. If you don't understand how to manage yourself, or how to model for others the meshing of emotional self-mastery with technical expertise and experience, you have no chance to motivate your staff or enable them to work together more constructively—especially during those critical moments when anxiety is peaking and productivity is collapsing. Anxious people do not think clearly: they perform very poorly in the workplace.

Decades ago, businessmen who were tough (read "abusive") to their staff used to be considered "shrewd." Anyone who cared about employees' emotions and concerns was considered "too soft" for management and faced a "glass ceiling" or a pink slip.

In recent decades these fallacies have been exposed for what they are: false notions based on a machismo culture. Fortunately, modern studies of human behavior demonstrate clearly that recognizing others' humanity is critical to increasing productivity, not a sign of weakness. We now know unequivocally that employees who are happy tend to stay in one place longer, and are more productive.

Thus, the concept of emotional competence is no longer seen as "softness" but accepted by academic and business mainstreams as a highly desired skill a leader and manager must possess to succeed.

I'm not suggesting that you buy the proverbial black leather couch and become a therapist to your staff, but emotional competence is a minimum qualification for any management or leadership position. Effective management elicits the best performance from people by understanding their needs and aspirations. Some people may respond well to deadline pressures and thrive on stress, while others need peace and quiet to do their best work. Most respond to some combination of both, and the same person may be more responsive to deadlines one day, but may need to retreat from office bustle the next.

Developing emotional competence is a learning process; anyone who possesses the native emotional intelligence and awareness that emotions can enhance or destroy one's ability to perform can become emotionally competent.

Bear in mind that a leader is also human and subject to the same emotions, concerns, yearnings, and ambitions that affect everyone else in the medical group. The big difference: you, as the leader, must exhibit greater self-control and take greater care in what you say publicly, and make certain that your tone and demeanor consistently reinforce your positive messages.

There are several sections in this book that focus on human resource management. In these sections you will be introduced to concepts that will help to enhance your emotional awareness and competence.

The book consists of two parts: Part I covers the sequence of activities required to launch a private medical practice (medical, dental, veterinary, chiropractic, etc.). Part II addresses ongoing management of the practice once it is up and running, including among others, the management of human resources, risks, and financial matters.

PART I: LAUNCHING THE PRACTICE

Part I of this book tracks a timeline—effectively a twelve-month countdown—culminating in the opening of a private practice. It's implicitly assumed that this is a solo or small practice consisting of a handful of doctors.

The timeline is meant to serve as a general guide for opening a practice in an existing building. If your intention is to construct a new purpose-built structure, you must allow additional time for acquiring the land and erecting the new building.

The twelve-month countdown, summarized in Figure 1, unfolds as follows:

1. A year in advance of the doors opening for business, **assemble your Accountant and Attorney** team (Hereafter I will refer to this as your **AA Team**)
2. Around the same time, begin to **scout out communities capable of supporting your practice.** (spend about 30 days on this activity)
3. Next, find a commercial real estate agent who has local knowledge of your preferred area, then **find a specific space and negotiate a lease** (spend about 30-60 days on this activity)
4. Around the same time frame as step 3, and in collaboration with your AA Team, **complete a business plan** and use that document to negotiate financing with a lender (spend about 30-60 days on this activity)

5. Next, begin to **assess and evaluate different technological solutions** (billing, client records, inventory management, accounting, credential management, etc.), (spend about 60 -90 days on this activity)
6. Over the same period of time as step 5, work with appropriate insurance agents to **identify and purchase needed insurance coverage** (malpractice, disability, health, life insurance, etc.), (spend about 30-60 days on this activity)
7. You should now be roughly half-way (6 months) to the doors opening for business. Over the next 3 months or so **identify and hire necessary support staff**
8. Over the same period as step 7, **order equipment and supplies,** and
9. **Make the necessary improvements to the existing location** (known as the *Build-out*) (typical build-out takes 90 days)
10. **Market your practice** well in advance of opening for business (spend at least 90 days on this activity, leading up to doors opening for business)
11. Several weeks in advance of opening for business, **train all staff members**. Ensure everyone is appropriately conversant with equipment and technological solutions, including software and hardware. In some cases, training may take place earlier (for example, if a vendor offers some special training or if there is a need for staff members to obtain certain licenses or qualifications in advance
12. **Open for business**

Depending on the nature of your specific practice, the order and duration of these timeline steps may require adjustment.

Subsequent chapters address each of these timeline components in greater detail.

It's advisable to contact your local (state or county) medical or dental society. These organizations often have useful resources and connections for private practitioners, including information on recent or pending legislation that may impact your business.

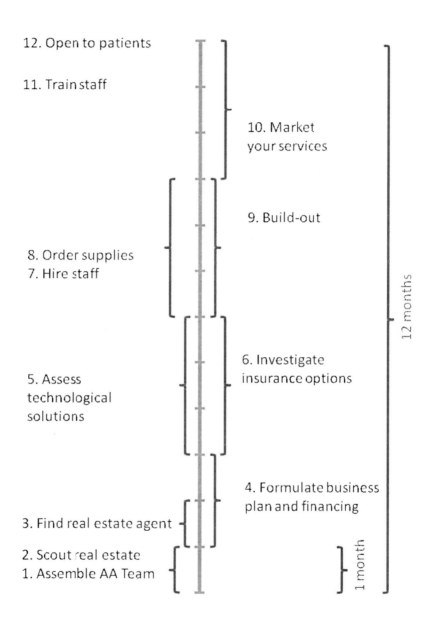

Figure 1: PRACTICE LAUNCH TIMELINE

Assemble the AA Team

The first step on the path to private practice is to form a team of experts. The core of the team must include an Accountant and an Attorney—hereafter "The AA Team". One of these will typically be the team leader. Both must have appropriate business skills and specialization in medical or dental practices.

These experts should offer relevant knowledge of the industry and local knowledge of providers and suppliers.

Broadly speaking, the attorney will review all contracts with suppliers, landlords, lenders, insurers, partners, and employees, and will also assist with regulatory compliance. The accountant will help with all business planning, tax filings, etc. The best professionals will also be able to provide you with business planning advice.

According to Allen Schiff, a CPA whose activities are dedicated to serving dental practices, practice owner(s) should sign an engagement letter with each of the CPA and attorney. In order to avoid any confusion or misunderstanding, each document should explicitly outline the terms of the agreement. For example:

1. Who is responsible for what
2. Level of service
3. Fees

The accountant and/or attorney will also help with introductions to other professional team members, including architects, real estate brokers, contractors, equipment suppliers, banks, and specialized technology solution providers (of billing, accounting, regulatory compliance and credential management software). There are those who suggest that team leaders should always provide more than one recommendation for each team vacancy, in order to avoid concerns about independence of recommendations. The doctor is then the one to make the final selections. This ensures that the doctor is involved in vetting all candidates (that level of involvement by doctors is sometimes referred to as "owning" the process).

The full team is likely to include at least the following:

1. Accountant
2. Attorney
3. Lender
4. Commercial real estate agent/broker/realtor
5. Design consultant/Architect
6. Equipment specialist
7. Insurance agent
8. Medical practice consultant

Because most legal and business considerations are local (state- and county-specific laws, state-specific accounting rules, local real estate expertise, local suppliers) it's highly advisable to form an AA Team in the vicinity of the intended practice. That is, if you are completing your education in New York and want to set up a practice in your hometown in California, your New York-based attorney and accountant should be replaced with a local California team. It's often useful to ask colleagues (physicians or dentists you know) in the intended location for attorney and accountant recommendations. All you need is to find one credible professional. That professional should then be able to help you identify the rest of the team. Interview each prospective professional to satisfy yourself that you feel comfortable and will be able to get along with him or her.

As a side note, you probably do need to say goodbye to your attorney when you move to a different state, because legal advice *must* be local (your attorney must be licensed to practice in your state and must be familiar with local laws). On the other hand, your primary accountant doesn't have to be local, although some local accounting presence may help under certain circumstances). So if you really like your existing accountant, you can probably continue that relationship.

Scout Out Locations for the Practice

Searching for a location is about much more than driving around and casually observing that a neighborhood looks nice. Selecting your neighborhood and the precise location within that neighborhood are among the most important decisions you need to make, and the process requires a rigorous approach. Fortunately, there are specialists who can help you generate and interpret demographic studies for proposed geographic areas. Prepare to pay for such information and keep in mind that it's sensible to spend money on this. You can initiate your own demographic examination, but it will take you much time—time you likely don't have. You also can't afford to make a mistake and select the wrong area.

Location, Location, Location!

According to Nathan Crowe, a commercial real estate broker specializing in medical services, doctors often neglect to closely examine reports providing insight into the demographic characteristics of their intended constituents. One such tool is a *Saturation Map*, which shows all competitors in a given region. This makes it easier to identify over- and under-served areas.

For example, a dermatologist may prefer an inexpensive suite costing $3 less per square foot than other locations but may not realize that the same building already houses six other dermatologists— it is *saturated*.

Another important demographic document is the *Payor Mix* report, which reflects the proportion of residents in a given area who are self-insured or covered under Medicare or Medicaid. Certain specialties lend themselves to certain mixes. For example, a high-end elective plastic surgery practice is less likely to succeed in an area where the majority of residents are covered under Medicaid.

Another important location consideration is where the patients are going to come from. Some specialties are tied to referrals from hospitals, and should therefore logically be situated in close proximity to hospitals. A cardiology practice may be a good example of this.

Other specialties do better in retail locations, and should therefore be closer to the community—in a shopping mall—or some other location with fairly heavy retail traffic. An example of this is an ophthalmologist, whose practice may be combined with retail sales of spectacles and contact lenses.

The scouting process should take about 30 days. It typically involves you suggesting several areas to the demographic firm, and receiving in return report(s) outlining the differences among the areas and identification of those that appear to be most favorable for your practice.

Secure Real Estate

Securing the correct real estate at the right price is one of your most important business decisions for at least two reasons:

- Location will influence how easily patients can find you and reach you. This will impact revenue generated
- You will likely be signing a five- to ten-year lease. This creates an extended and large financial obligation on your part, which can easily add up to hundreds of thousands of dollars of fixed costs over the course of several years

Some considerations when evaluating property:

1. The demographics of the neighborhood must be sufficient to support your specialty
2. The location must be easily accessible, should lend itself to comfortable foot traffic and have sufficient parking (if patients can't find parking, they'll find a new doctor)
3. The facility must be the correct size for your proposed operations, and allow for anticipated growth. (But you don't want to lease too much space. There's no point in paying for space you won't be using)
4. It must have the correct physical features for your practice specialty. For example, dental offices require deeper spaces between floors to house oversized pipes and electric cables

5. You want a good landlord—one who will be fair and responsive
6. You need permission to advertise within and outside the facility
7. The price has to be right—don't overpay
8. If you are moving from another facility, it's helpful if the new location allows for easy transport of your existing equipment
9. Can you get an option for another extended period (5-10 years) to protect against having to move and rebuild the practice elsewhere? You may even be able to build-in maximum rate increases on that optional term, giving you greater certainty about future rent expenses

Get a Good Real Estate Agent Who Acts on Your Behalf

Doctors tend to underestimate the importance of working with a commercial real estate agent. Sometimes they don't understand the realtor's job function, or they may feel they will have more control over negotiations on their own, or they question the realtor's motives, or they want to save money by not paying a realtor.

While doctors are unquestionably intelligent people, their experience is medical—they spend their time providing excellent services to their patients. Doctors don't spend their time with their finger on the proverbial pulse of the local real estate market. As pointed out by Charles Feitel, a realtor specializing in medical and dental practices, in general doctors have a very limited sense of the: available inventory of properties, what the *improvement allowance* should be (the amount of money the landlord will spend to prepare the space for you), and what fair market rents are for specific areas. This is not due to lack of intellect—it is simply due to a lack of time to commit to becoming expert at the complex and dynamic world of real estate.

Medical real estate is different from traditional office space, so it's important to work with a specialized realtor. A good one will know exactly where all the vacant former medical spaces are in your area of interest. These facilities are much more likely to have the correct plumbing and electrical wiring already in place, along with other practice-specific features. For example, in a dental suite, the plumbing must be in the middle of the room (in a regular office location the plumbing is accessible through a wall—the edge of a room).

Landlords may try to attract doctors by offering to convert regular office space (at great expense), but it's more efficient to go with a realtor who can find existing space that already has the specialized facilities. This allows you to open up shop faster and to spend more of your money on final touches or better equipment, or to pay more to secure the services of a good billing expert or administrator.

Being in a medical services building presents other advantages: you may find neighbors (other medical practitioners) who can provide you with patient referrals. But, of course, you wouldn't want to be in a building full of people with the same specialty as yours. Your realtor should be aware of this.

What doctors often don't realize is that if you hire the realtor, she has a fiduciary duty to you. Thus, the realtor is on your side and is obligated by law to give you the best advice for your circumstances. In contrast, a realtor who is hired by a landlord owes allegiance to the landlord. You should ensure that your working relationship is one that imposes a fiduciary duty on your realtor. Discuss this upfront with all candidates and choose a realtor who: explicitly acknowledges the fiduciary duty to you, has direct experience representing medical practitioners, and has intimate knowledge of the local market.

Another misconception has to do with who pays the realtor. Generally, the realtor is paid by the landlord (once the deal is struck). You don't pay the realtor.

Have your AA Team attorney examine the realtor's proposed working agreement. Because your attorney is paid by the hour, it tends to be advisable to first vet the realtor candidates on your own and send only the finalist's proposed contract to your attorney. If you interview four realtors and send all their contracts to the attorney, you will be charged for four contract reviews. Doing an initial screen on the realtor candidates could save you money, but even more importantly, you will learn a lot from conversing with them.

You should get your AA Team's opinion on the proposed lease agreement from the landlord, but it can be a mistake to get your attorney or accountant directly involved in detailed real estate negotiations. Yes, a knowledgeable AA Team can provide useful input, but those billable negotiation hours can add up quickly. The point is that a good realtor who understands your business and owes you a fiduciary duty (and whom you don't have to pay) could instead be negotiating expertly on your behalf. This is even more compelling if your AA Team lacks specific knowledge of the local real estate market.

A very common mistake doctors make is failing to allow enough lead time for the real estate search. As noted earlier in the timeline discussion, it's generally wise to allow a full year for the process to play out. This allows you to take your time and do your homework at every step. You can deal proactively with any roadblocks along the way (for example, having to switch contractors, or needing extra time to obtain occupancy agreements from the county or finalize registrations with insurers). The alternative is to be constantly under time pressure, and being forced to make sub-par decisions or cut corners to meet various deadlines.

Giving yourself ample time applies to your initial real estate search but also as you approach renewal on an existing location's lease. Give yourself a full year to become reacquainted with real estate market conditions around your practice area, and most importantly, send a clear signal to your exiting landlord that you are proactively looking for better alternatives. This gives you the greatest negotiating leverage over the landlord. If you leave the decision until two months before your current lease expires your landlord has you over the proverbial barrel. He knows you don't have time to find an alternative, putting him in position to force you to accept unfavorable terms. Even worse, you may find yourself stuck in a drastically (and unfavorably) changed demographic situation.

According to Charles Feitel, many leases specify that if you don't renew, you become a *holdover tenant*. Under a holdover tenancy you may only be required to give thirty days' notice, but your monthly rent may double! Landlords use the threat of holdover tenancy to force renewals, but it's better for all concerned to avoid lapsing into this scenario.

You can avoid all this by having your realtor contact the landlord 9-12 months in advance of the lease expiration. The landlord will immediately know: that you have professional, well-informed representation, that you will be able to easily assess the fairness of proposed renewal terms given current market conditions, and that you have a credible threat to leave if you aren't happy with renewal terms. This should make the process quick and even-sided.

Why should you use the realtor at renewal? Can't you simply contact the landlord directly, well in advance of renewal?

Yes, you could do that, but keep in mind that you won't be paying the realtor for her time—she will be paid by the landlord. Furthermore, the realtor will be able to use her market knowledge to secure a good deal. Some less favorable outcomes are described in these two examples, set during a time when rental rates had dropped:

Example 1: Doctor 1, currently paying $40 per square foot (psf), approached his landlord directly to discuss renewal. The landlord offered renewal at $38 psf. The doctor happily accepted, and immediately called his spouse to celebrate his negotiating brilliance.

Example 2: Doctor 2, currently also paying $40 psf approached her landlord directly to discuss renewal. The landlord offered renewal at $38 psf. After having her attorney review the offer and negotiate on her behalf, the landlord agreed to reduce the rate to $35 psf. The doctor triumphantly called her spouse to celebrate.

What neither of the doctors realized was that the going market rate at time of re-negotiation was $33 psf. Doctor 2 also had to pay her attorney $5,000 in fees for assistance in the lease negotiation.

The morals of these stories are that you should never accept the first offer made by the landlord, and you should always have your negotiations handled by an expert who knows the correct (fair) market prices.

Another common error by medical practitioners is focusing too heavily on reducing upfront costs.

Most landlords will give a big improvement allowance to new tenants, but fall short of paying for the full medical build-out. Doctors often try to minimize upfront cost by scaling back the build-out (known as "value-engineering" the build-out plan). This is often self-defeating. Doctors don't move every 2-3 years: they sign long-term leases (at least 7-year and sometimes 10-year leases). Accordingly, they should average out the extra costs over that longer-term lease period, and recognize that the full build-out may well create a more comfortable environment for patients. (The process of averaging costs over a long period is known as *amortizing*).

By skimping or cutting back on finishes, they are hurting future business potential. Making the space comfortable and inviting helps to attract and retain patients. That is money well spent. Shortcuts lead to sterile environments. Patients are much more likely to come back and to refer friends to a comfortable and attractive location. A sterile, bare, or cheap atmosphere reflects poorly on the practice.

Another important consideration is that you should not be required to begin paying rent during the build-out phase. You should only be required to do so once you are open for business and realistically in position to earn revenue to pay the rent. This should be explicitly stated in the lease agreement. Look for the terms defining the Lease Commencement Date. Additional details on this are provided in the Practice Design and Build-out chapter.

Nathan Crowe also suggests that working with a specialized architect who understands patient flow can be important. The flow in a medical office is not the same as that in regular office space.

The Landlord's Perspective

In effect, when you sign a 10-year lease you are "marrying" the landlord. For better or worse, for richer or poorer, your fortunes are tied together. It therefore behooves you to understand the landlord's perspective on your relationship.

Some doctors think that they can save money or curry favor by dealing directly with the landlord. But this can be bad for several reasons:

- The landlord does not have a fiduciary duty to you, so if he can arrange a deal that is better for him (and worse for you) he will happily do so
- The landlord spends every hour of every day negotiating and deal making, and the landlord knows a lot about the local real estate market. A doctor may be intelligent and highly capable, but simply doesn't have the same number of negotiating hours under his belt, and lacks knowledge of local real estate markets and norms. Don't make it a point of ego to try to beat the landlord. It's a waste of your time and money

Some doctors think that cutting out the commercial real estate broker and dealing with the landlord directly gives more leverage. Their logic is that the landlord doesn't need to pay a broker, and some of those savings can be passed onto the doctor. But the landlord can easily make sure the extra savings benefit him instead of you. Without the benefit of a broker acting in a fiduciary duty on your behalf, you are at a big disadvantage.

Perhaps the most surprising observation for doctors is that landlords don't want to work with them directly. Why? Because the typical medical practice is small, requiring less than 1,000 square feet of space. This makes it relatively insignificant to a landlord seeking to rent out 500,000 square feet of space. For many landlords, it simply isn't practical to spend a lot of time communicating with, educating and negotiating directly with an individual doctor. Add to this the prevailing stereotype that doctors are overly demanding, arrogant, and don't do their homework, and you can see why landlords prefer to work through real estate brokers.

Formulate Business Plan & Financing

First, what exactly is a business plan?

A *Business Plan* is the detailed written explanation of how you intend to provide valuable services to patients and achieve success. *Success* is defined in terms of meeting explicit short-, medium-, and long-term objectives.

Why do you need such a plan?

A business plan is necessary for at least three reasons:

1. The process of putting together the plan (along with solid numerical estimates for revenues, expenses, and profits) helps to confirm your resolve and commitment to owning a practice, with all the responsibilities that entails
2. Putting together the plan forces you to think carefully about many crucial issues. It's far better to think about these in advance and plan for them carefully, rather than trying to deal with them in *ad hoc* fashion later
3. The plan helps you come across as level-headed, credible, committed, grounded, driven, and responsible. If you can't make this impression, you can forget about getting any lender to give you money

The harsh facts are that a lender doesn't care whether you graduated near the top (or bottom) of your class, or whether you are a brilliant dermatologist or talented pediatric dentist. The lender cares about whether you can run a successful business and pay back the amount you borrowed plus interest. Similarly, suppliers will only extend credit once they are convinced that you are a responsible, level-headed business person. These impressions can be made (or unmade) based on the sophistication and accuracy of your business plan.

Value Proposition and Mission Statement

A business plan usually includes a mission statement and value proposition.

These two items are sometimes dismissed as shallow statements that might be made by a beauty pageant contestant ("I want my magical new company to wipe out all sickness globally and give everyone in the world perfect teeth.") But undertaken thoughtfully, these two statements can be very powerful, providing focus and helping to communicate your intentions to staff and patients. They can also be used to explain how your practice differs from competitor offerings. Both statements are crucial to competing successfully and growing your practice.

Mission Statement: The *Mission Statement* is the explanation of the firm's *raison d'etre* ("reason for being"), stated as simply, concisely and eloquently as possible.

You should select staff with the skills, integrity and inclination to match the Mission Statement and its underlying values. For example, if your Mission is excellent client service, seek people with outstanding client service abilities. Build the Mission into company culture: tie performance goals and incentive pay to excellent customer service.

If your Mission is to apply ground-breaking new medical technologies to explore new treatments, then you should hire like-minded people, and equip them with cutting-edge equipment.

If the Mission Statement is not uniformly embraced, it's meaningless. Its absence leaves a vacuum, along with confused employees who are unsure what their greater purpose is. This lack of certainty means they will be tentative in the workplace, without a strong conviction to guide them and their decisions.

Value Proposition: A *Value Proposition* emphasizes what your firm can uniquely do for the patient population, and differentiates your solutions from competitors' offerings. It's usually service and market segment-specific. This means you may need a separate value proposition for each client segment or major service offering. Write Value Proposition(s) in compelling, positive language to set your company apart.

When you first look at a well-written Value Proposition, you may think "Well, duh!" because it seems so simple, so obvious—but there should be some profundity there.

Profound, elegant, and compelling statements are challenging to articulate, but well worth the time. The process calls for deep, insightful, and forward-looking understanding of patient needs (often before they realize those needs), then offering a solution that solves real problems.

As noted earlier, an "all purpose" one-size-fits-all Value Proposition will not be compelling unless you have just one product, one service, or one patient type.

If you do have just one client base or service offering, go through the process of imagining how to diversify your offerings and customer base. This can be an excellent "brainstorming" technique which can lead you to identify new prospective patient markets, study their needs, and sell your services.

Consider the following questions:

- How should patient segments be defined?
- How many distinct segments are there?
- What unique needs does each segment have?
- Do you have offerings to meet more of these needs?
- Is it cost-efficient to target many, or only a few, segments?
- Given the importance of focus and impact, which patient segments are most critical and deserve your earliest attention?

You must understand the characteristics of each client segment to answer these questions.

Understanding patient characteristics and needs requires documenting, through meaningful personal contact, the key elements of each service your practice provides. You should embrace feedback from all staff members, beginning with the moment the patient picks up the phone or walks in the door, to the final goodbyes at the end of treatment. This means soliciting feedback from receptionists, nurses, interns, doctors and administrators.

This process, done correctly, imposes much-needed discipline, and forces teams to set aside old assumptions and answer questions from a fresh and open-minded perspective. You may realize certain existing services have to be altered, delivered differently, or terminated. Building a successful practice that addresses patient needs correctly requires this clarity and pragmatism, and may call for additional staff development.

The very act of formulating a Mission Statement and Value Proposition(s) is constructive, as it gets everyone thinking carefully about what you ultimately want to achieve.

Your AA Team should be able to provide you with a lot of guidance on putting together a business plan. According to Allen Schiff, it's advisable to adhere to some version of the following outline.

Business Plan Outline

This outline assumes you are a brand new startup business seeking a loan. Some of the information may differ if you have an existing practice and are seeking to expand or open a new location, or seeking to buy an existing practice.

- Executive summary stating why you need the loan, how much you need, your revenue and expense estimates over at least the next five years, and why you and your team are certain you will be successful

- List of management team members including biographies and detailed CVs establishing appropriate credibility in the area you intend to practice. Include information about medical practitioners and as many AA Team members as possible, such as the CPA, attorney, and practice management consultant. It's especially important to list those providing business management guidance as this is traditionally the skill most often missing from aspiring medical practices—and the one lenders will look for

- List of other employees (clerical and support staff) and their related job responsibilities and rates of pay
- Brief overview of the practice including area(s) of specialty, the types of services to be delivered, estimated number of employees, forecasted number of clients, and business organization choice (LLC, S-Corp, C-Corp, etc.)
- Value proposition addressing the questions: why should patients come to me instead of going to a competitor? What is the unique value my practice will provide to its clients?
- Details of what the loan proceeds will be used for, including a breakdown of all major equipment purchases or leases and related costs
- Outline of the anticipated build-out requirements and associated costs, including estimates from architects and or contractors
- Collateral available to secure the loan (for a brand new business the lender may require posting of personal collateral—for example, your personal residence, a life and/or disability insurance policy)
- Demographic reports establishing that the location makes sense and that the local community can be reasonably expected to support the practice
- Analysis of the existing or forecasted competition in your market area
- Evidence that registration has either been completed or is pending with appropriate insurers
- Evidence that registration has either been completed or is pending with appropriate regulatory bodies
- Description of marketing plan(s) to be implemented, and in the event you intend to use a marketing firm, its contact information
- Risk analysis identifying the dangers faced by the practice along with plans to mitigate those risks and vulnerabilities
- Financial statements (balance sheets and income statements) with at least three years and ideally five years of forecasts

The lender will likely also request your personal credit report as well as several of your most recent income tax returns.

Financing Sources

When it comes to financing your new practice you almost always need a loan to cover the purchase of equipment, pay initial salaries and rent, and cover the costs of attorneys, accountants, architects, practice consultants, etc. Depending on your medical specialty, the amount borrowed may range from $200,000 to $600,000 or more. You effectively have two lender choices:

1. Banks that don't have specialized health care lending units. These are usually smaller, local banks
2. Banks with specialized health care departments. These are usually found in larger banks such as Citibank, Bank of America, PNC, etc., although some smaller banks do participate in this niche

It's often better to deal with the second group: specialist lenders who understand your circumstances instead of a local bank that doesn't. The specialist bank understands that you will have a lot of debt and little income early on, but also that you have a potentially powerful future income stream. In contrast, the local or non-specialist bank may require that you post personal assets as collateral or provide other guarantees that a specialist will not demand. It may also charge you higher interest for a loan. Why will this happen? The non-specialist bank sets worse terms for the doctor primarily due to its own ignorance. Banks charge you based on your perceived risk, if they don't fully understand your business, they are forced to do the conservative thing, which is to assume you fall into a riskier borrower category, and charge you more. The local bank often falls into this less knowledgeable category, whereas the specialist lender is less concerned because its officers are more familiar with your particular business.

Gareth Petsch, who heads Citi Commercial Bank's Healthcare Solutions Group, says that his clients borrow anywhere from $250,000 to $10,000,000. The most typical loans range from $750,000 to $5,000,000.

Deals processed by Citibank's specialized unit include startup financing, extension financing, buy-ins, buy-outs, loans for acquiring real estate, cash flow consolidation, succession planning, and exit strategy financing. The basic driver of activity is lending, but the bank's staff can also provide some consulting assistance.

For startups, doctors often have incorrect expectations about costs and projected revenues—the forecasts included in doctors' business plans are usually overly optimistic. In fairness, this optimism is present in almost every forecast in any business—*irrational exuberance* is not exclusive to doctors. As an example, when I was a corporate executive in New York City, I was approached by an Atlanta-based startup seeking to sell its shares to a deep-pocketed investor. The owners of the startup asked that I approve a deal valuing their firm at 500 million dollars. Needless to say, the answer was (a polite) 'no.' Two years later the same owners contacted me, sheepishly suggested that they must have been under the influence of recreational drugs when they came up with the original number, and explained that they'd consider an offer in the 5 million dollar range.

Specialist banks (as well as experienced AA Team members) can give doctors historical benchmarks to help get their business plan numbers in line. For example, there are benchmarks by specialty on how many patients must be seen daily to reach certain revenue thresholds. And there are benchmarks on the maximum number of patients you can realistically see daily. A fast way to lose credibility with a lender (or any business partner) is to submit unrealistic forecasts. Before you present the bank with numbers, your specialized accountant should help you kick the tires and ensure your numbers are realistic and support your arguments.

Putting together financial statements is not just a mechanical exercise. You need to fully understand what the numbers imply. Here's an example courtesy of accountant Samuel Luxenburg who was approached by a physician whose loan applications were all summarily rejected by lenders. A quick review provided the answer: the physician didn't realize that the forecasts he submitted projected losses every year!

The broader message here is that as a business owner you should know your accounting (numbers) inside out, including the business implications of those numbers. This level of enlightenment is referred to as "owning the numbers" and is crucial because it allows you to make good decisions and take effective action.

Build-out Financing Choices

According to Nathan Crowe, doctors tend to underutilize a financing option available to them, and end up cutting corners in the build-out of their practice. This leaves them with a facility that is less than ideal and therefore less effective.

Here is a specific example: consider a doctor seeking to set up shop in a 2,000 square foot (sf) facility. The doctor is offered a 10-year lease at $35 per square foot (psf) a year, and a one-time $60 psf improvements allowance by the landlord. In other words, the landlord will pay for the first $60 psf of build-out improvements, and the doctor will be responsible for covering any additional costs. In dollar terms, the landlord is offering a total of $60 psf x 2,000 sf = $120,000.

The doctor has also been told by his contractor that the ideal build-out requested by the doctor will cost $80 psf—a total expenditure of $160,000. Thus, the doctor will be responsible out of pocket for $40,000 of improvement expenses ($160,000 − $120,000).

The doctor decides to cut corners on the build-out. He scales the plans back until the revised build-out expenses are at $120,000, matching the landlord's allowance.

This may make sense in some cases but in others the doctor may be shooting himself in the foot. The corner-cutting may lead to inadequate plumbing, an uninviting reception area, poor lighting, a flawed paint job, low quality cabinetry that will have to be replaced, or any number of other deficiencies that reduce revenue and/or increase costs.

Instead, the doctor could have proceeded with the full (ideal) build-out and financed those additional improvements (costing $40,000) with a loan, payable over a ten year period. Using a financial calculator and a 5% rate of interest on the loan, let's assume the annual expense for paying back the loan would be $2.54 psf per year, or $2.54 x 10 years x 2,000 sf = $50,800 over ten years. The $2.54 would be an additional expense above and beyond the $35 psf charged by the landlord.

This is not a very large amount in the grand scheme of things, and may well be worth it to create the ideal environment that proves more attractive to patients.

It is often better to get financing for such build-outs from a (specialized) bank rather than from a landlord. Landlords may offer to lend directly to a tenant to cover the tenants' share of improvement expenses, but may do so at higher interest rates, say at 8% instead of the 5% available from a specialized lender.

The landlord may also offer to add the financed portion of improvement costs to the annual base rent ($35 + $2.54 = $37.54). This can be even worse for the tenant. Why? Because typical leases allow the landlord to raise the rent every year by some inflation adjustment amount, often around 3%. Including the financed amount of $2.54 in the base rent would mean that each year as the base rent amount increases by 3%, the tenant would pay an extra 3% on each dollar of financing costs. The next year the rent would again go up by 3%, compounding the cost of the financing by the inflation adjustment.

In this case it is clear that the doctor would be better off electing the specialized bank financing rather than borrowing from the landlord, but to be sure, you should go through the numbers or deputize one of your AA Team members to do that for you.

Personal Credit Management

Another consideration when it comes to financing is the need to responsibly manage one's personal credit. Gareth Petsch cautions that some doctors are "too casual and nonchalant" about maintaining a good credit history. They may not fully understand that lenders look very closely at how a prospective borrower has dealt with credit card and student debt. A person who shows a disciplined record of on-time payments is viewed favorably. One who misses payments is viewed as lacking personal discipline and character. While this may be unfair to a medical student or resident who is struggling to cover all expenses on a very small salary, it is nevertheless the way judgments are made by lenders and credit score providers.

Banks rely heavily on individual *credit scores* when making personal and small business loans. According to bankrate.com: "Your credit score is a three-digit number generated by a mathematical algorithm using information in your credit report. It's designed to predict risk, specifically, the likelihood that you will become seriously delinquent on your credit obligations in the 24 months after scoring."

There are many algorithms in use today; by far the most dominant is the one produced by FICO. FICO scores range from 300 to 850. Higher numbers represent more favorable scores (lower credit risk).

Credit reports are produced by the three major credit bureaus: Equifax, Experian and TransUnion. By law, you have a right to view your credit report (from each agency) for free once a year. Note that you have a right to view each credit *report* for free—not the actual *scores*.

Doctors should review their own credit scores periodically (at least annually) to ensure they know what those scores are, and whether they have deteriorated for any reason. Scores can be obtained from the aforementioned credit bureaus or directly from myFICO.com. If scores have declined significantly, it's important to take steps to resuscitate them by making good on any late payments, and requesting corrections in cases where records are erroneous.

The first line of defense when it comes to credit is responsible borrowing and spending. Don't borrow too much. Live within your means. Pay bills on time. Be aware that too many credit card accounts can hurt your score. Maintaining balances too close to maximum limits can hurt your score as well. Many online sources provide information on how to protect and repair one's credit score.

Keep in mind that credit scores depend on:

1. Payment history, and especially missed payments. You may be forgiven a single negative event, but a pattern of missed or late payments will hurt you. Paying two days late is better than paying 20 days late
2. The amount you owe on each account, especially if those amounts are close to the maximum limits
3. How long each account has been open
4. The account mix: the number and types of accounts (revolving credit such as credit cards, installment credit such as car loans, etc.)
5. New accounts opened or sought (yes, the mere indication that you are interested in opening a new account can be held against you). So don't open any accounts you don't need, especially if you are about to ask for an important source of credit, for example, a home mortgage

Keep these factors in mind and tailor your behavior to maximize your scores.

Collateral

After reviewing your credit score(s) and business plan, the bank will also evaluate the quality of your available collateral. What constitutes acceptable collateral to a financial institution? The answer is: any asset that the bank can take ownership of and sell to recoup money lent to a delinquent borrower. Real estate owned by the borrower is the most obvious example of collateral. In some cases, it is actually easier to obtain a loan to purchase real estate for your practice than it is to obtain funding for renting real estate. Why? Because in the former case the real estate can be seized by the bank if the business defaults. In the latter case (real estate is leased) the lender can't take ownership of the real estate and must instead rely on other assets pledged by the borrower (which often include furniture and equipment with low resale values).

Another asset the bank may accept as collateral is "Receivables." *Receivables* are the payments you are expecting to receive from your patients. If the bank has confidence that your clients will pay you, it may agree to lend to you after laying claim to those future receipts. The more stable and predictable your receipts, the more likely the bank is to accept them as collateral. If you are just starting out and have few or no patients, the receivables will be small and unreliable, likely prompting the bank to refuse them as collateral.

Generally, you are most disadvantaged if you are looking to lease, have high student debt, and no history of income generation. In such cases the bank may demand that you pledge personal assets as collateral. Acceptable collateral may include your home, car, the cash value in a life insurance policy, a non-qualified investment account, or any other personal asset the bank feels it can turn into cash.

One type of asset the bank will not consider is a *qualified investment account* such as a 401(k), 403(b), or IRA account. Why is that? A bank cannot legally seize qualified accounts, and if it can't get its hands on such accounts, it won't consider them in your application. Ironically, a doctor who has worked in a hospital for ten years prior to setting up a private practice may have hundreds of thousands of dollars in a qualified 401(k) account, but this asset will be effectively ignored by the prospective lending institution. This brings us back to the discussion in Book I regarding living within your means and putting excess money aside in a savings account or building up cash value in a life insurance policy. Either alternative can help you develop a store of money you can use for: a rainy day (emergency), as a down payment on a big purchase, or to establish collateral for a loan. (Building up cash value in a permanent insurance policy can take many years. Permanent policies are complex. See Book I for details).

Risk Exposures

Banks want assurances that doctors understand their own practices' vulnerabilities. They want to see that the owner/doctor is planning for the *what if* scenarios which may include illness, injury or death. Many medical practitioners fail to ask *what if*, and have no contingency plans in place. "A solo practitioner is at greatest risk. Every day [a] practice is closed it loses value tremendously, it walks over a cliff" says Petsch. In contrast, in a group practice, if one doctor passes away or becomes disabled or decides to leave for some reason, the others can pitch-in to keep the practice afloat and ensure that it retains value and viability.

Whether you are a solo practitioner or working as part of a group, it's imperative that all doctors arrange for life and disability insurance, and adopt a succession plan and/or buy-sell agreement specifying mechanisms for dealing with ownership changes.

Here's a real story of a solo practitioner with a successful practice, a wife and two babies. The family had a mortgage on their home as well as debts on the medical practice. The doctor did not have sufficient life insurance, no disability insurance and no Will. He was killed in a car accident, leaving the family to deal with intense grief and debts in excess of $800,000. The practice was sold for $200,000 in a fire sale, leaving his grieving widow with $600,000 in debt and 2 babies to care for. She subsequently lost the family home because she couldn't afford to pay the mortgage.

This example was the most painful one I had to document for this book, for two reasons: it's a tragic story, but most importantly from an educator's perspective, it's a situation that should never have happened. This sad outcome was completely avoidable through the use of simple and affordable insurance products (discussed in Book I and later in this book). Either the lender or the physician's financial advisor could have realized that insurance was needed.

In addition to managing risks by demanding that medical practices are properly insured, banks like to be approached by credible management teams with broad skill sets. They will likely assess whether the borrowers are insisting on doing everything themselves, or relying on expert lawyers, accountants and administrators to make solid business decisions. It's much cheaper to hire good advisors than to clean up a mess later on. This wisdom is occasionally lost on medical practitioners who fail to realize that they themselves lack certain business skills and that skimping on a few thousand dollars early on can lead to much steeper legal and business liabilities later. You may recognize this as a common refrain throughout the *Pillars of Wealth* series—doctors often cut corners because they are too busy or over-confident, and these decisions come back to haunt them.

Banking Services

Beyond lending, banks provide a variety of other services you may wish to utilize. In fact, the bank will likely automatically open a checking account for you when you are approved for the business loan. You may also be given the option of a savings account and a credit card.

The bank may also offer small business services, including handling your firm's payroll needs, and the ability for your business to accept credit card payments from clients.

Find someone you trust at your financial institution and develop a good personal relationship with that person. Do this even if you prefer online banking. Your human contact can help you navigate the complex institution and get you to the specialists much more effectively (and with significantly less frustration) than calling an 800 number in search of answers.

Most banks assign private bankers or relationship managers to preferred clients. A doctor's earning capacity should qualify you for that extra level of attention. Take advantage of it.

Third Party Financing

Third party financing refers to agreements with third party lenders to finance medical procedures for patients. (In case you're wondering, you and your patient are the first and second parties).

Some third party lenders are CareCredit™ GE Capital Retail Bank, AccessOne®, and American Healthcare Lending. Third party lending can be used to pay for procedures that are not covered by health insurance. Some of these may include: dental care, eyeglasses, contacts, LASIK, hearing care, veterinary services, and cosmetic surgery.

The mechanism is typically as follows: Your practice puts the patient in touch with the third party lender (your staff may help the client to complete the application forms). Once approved, the third party lender pays you the entire amount minus a service fee. The patient ends up with a credit card account that has the full cost of the procedure charged to it upfront.

Subsequently, the patient pays off the debt to the lender in monthly payments. The patient may be required to pay interest monthly, or under certain conditions, the lender may offer special promotions including zero interest over some specified period (for example, 12 or 18 months). These promotions often have very strict rules, so patients may find themselves having to pay very large interest penalties in the event they breach the rules. It's advisable that you (or your staff) warn clients in advance about the downside of not meeting promotion guidelines.

The benefits to participating in third party financing are that you are paid upfront and never have to chase the patient down over a delinquent payment. This allows you to focus on what you do best—delivering high quality medical services. For these reasons, it may make a lot of sense to incorporate third party financing into your business plan.

Assess and Select Technological Solutions

It should come as no surprise that technological solutions play a big role in the success of a private practice. Properly adopted, technology efficiently enables a broad spectrum of activities or functions, helping to increase productivity and lower costs.

As soon as you make the decision to pursue private practice, you should strive to familiarize yourself with the typical solutions offered in support of your intended specialty. Read about these solutions, ask medical practice consultants about them, and/or visit a friend's practice to see them in use.

Many companies will happily *demo* (demonstrate) their tools for you, in some cases giving you free access to the tools for a limited period of time. Take advantage of these free trial opportunities to better understand which software features are available and most important to your practice.

According to David Kovel, Chief Information Officer at Sage Growth Partners, a technology company focused on the health care industry, the automated health care practice is usually facilitated by the following information systems:

1. Practice Management system (PM) – a system for patient registration, scheduling, insurance billing, and accounts receivable management. A good billing system is the lifeline of your business—don't underestimate its importance. More on billing in a subsequent chapter

2. Electronic Medical Records system (EMR) – a system for storing each patient's clinical data, also enabling electronic prescription writing and order tracking
3. Document Management system – a system for storing scanned or faxed documents. Often, this capability is a component of the EMR system
4. Patient Portal – a secured, external website that enables direct electronic interaction with the practice's patients.
5. Office Automation software – word processing, spreadsheet, and electronic mail system to enable internal and external communication
6. Accounting software – general business accounting software used to manage the business' books, cash flow, and to facilitate tax reporting
7. Management Analytics software – tools to facilitate analysis of the efficiency of the business

Prior to adopting any system you must ensure it will cover your practice's needs. You should begin with a process known as *requirements gathering*. As the name implies, this involves gathering a list of all the functions or requirements you will want the technological solution to perform. Once you have that list, you can evaluate whether a given software product will meet your needs.

To facilitate requirements gathering, you should use real life case studies reflecting the actual needs in your practice. For example, map out the entire process of getting a patient signed in to the practice, all the steps involved in treatment, all the staff members who come into contact with the patient or the patient's records, all the types of materials that may be used in providing the medical service to the patient, all the interactions with insurers, etc. Tracking all these activities through a real case will enable you to identify the different pieces of information your software must capture and store, and the various analytical measurements the software must calculate.

David Kovel points out that for very complex system requirements, it may make sense to issue a formal *request for proposal* (RFP) to various software providers. The RFP should clearly identify all features the software must have in order to meet your needs. Ideally, you want several software providers to submit competing bids to produce your software as this will help to keep the price reasonable. You can then choose the provider that suggests the best solution. Keep in mind that the best solution does not necessarily mean the cheapest solution.

In addition, you must evaluate the software based on its *total cost of ownership* (TCO). That is, don't just focus on the first-year cost of software installation. Rather, consider all other related costs, including ongoing maintenance costs, salaries to specialized staff who may be needed to maintain the system(s), training of existing staff, cost of any additional hardware that may be required (for example, servers, printers, etc.), and costs to connect the new system(s) to existing ones.

In some cases, it may make sense to hire technical support staff to maintain the system in-house. In other cases it will make more sense to outsource technical management of the software and hardware to an external *managed service organization* (MSO).

Involving your staff early on (beginning with the original requirements gathering phase) is crucial for at least two reasons:

1. To ensure you properly identify all the functions the software must perform
2. To get staff members involved and enthusiastic about the new system

An all-too-common outcome when it comes to bringing in a new technology system is that staff members resent having to learn to do things differently, and in some cases feel threatened by the new system. A natural response under such circumstances is to not use the system fully, or to ignore it completely. Needless to say, this means your practice won't realize the intended efficiencies and will instead have spent large amounts of time and money for nothing.

Fully train the staff prior to deploying the new system. Keep in mind that just because the training classes have taken place, doesn't necessarily mean the learning has been achieved. Here's an example from a lab technician in an ophthalmology practice that rolled out a new electronic medical record system. She was required to sit through 14 training classes. After the first few she was utterly frustrated and wanted to quit the job, despite having worked at the practice for six years. When the practice managers debriefed her after the initial training sessions, they decided to take bold action and demanded that a new teacher be assigned by the technology company. After the change, the lab technician was able to learn what was needed and came to appreciate the new solution.

It's nice to have stories with happy endings, but in this case that outcome hinged on the open mindedness and commitment by management to ensure that the training was effective. Such stories often don't have happy endings.

Getting the right technology systems in place can make your life a lot easier and your practice more profitable. But this does require commitment of time—much of it upfront in the form of requirements gathering and identification of the best technology partner. The more complex your systems, the more conscientious you must be in monitoring their performance to ensure they are working properly. Consider annual reviews of your systems and keep in mind that as technology evolves, your practice should consider doing the same.

A final thought regarding the adoption of new technological solutions. Unless you are highly interested and/or savvy when it comes to new hardware or software—don't buy the first version of anything. Instead, wait for products to be market-tested, so all the kinks and bugs can be ironed-out. It's tough enough to run a medical/dental practice with all its associated complexities. It's doubly tough to run a practice and simultaneously struggle with poorly performing or misunderstood technology products. So let others be the first adopters and beta testers, while you focus on what you do best—delivering excellent medical services.

Assess & Purchase Insurance

In this book our focus is on the use of insurance products by businesses. In Book 1 of the *Pillars of Wealth* series (*Personal Finance Essentials for Medical Professionals*) the focus was on personal insurance (for individual doctors and their families).

Book I sets the stage for our current discussion by covering: the guidelines for identifying solid insurance companies, the key features and terminology of insurance products, and the basic types of insurance (property & casualty, disability, life, medical malpractice, and long term care).

We now turn our attention to two categories of insurance products for businesses: insurance to protect employees (group insurance) and insurance to protect the business itself.

Group Insurance

Your business can purchase *group insurance* policies which provide coverage to your employees. These are often positioned as part of a comprehensive benefits package. Generally, group policies are similar to their personal counterparts: there are annual premiums, deductibles, coverage limits, and coverage exclusions. However, group insurance coverage ends when an employee leaves the company.

Another difference with group plans is that health testing may be unnecessary. For example, when an employee becomes eligible for group life or disability insurance through a company—that employee may not be required to undergo a physical exam or blood test. Rather, coverage is automatic as long as the employee meets basic requirements such as being a full-time employee or fulfilling some probationary period.

How can insurance companies afford not to medically test people covered in group plans? Simple: insurance companies are all about risk diversification. A diverse pool of employees ensures that on average only a small number of people will manifest severe health issues. While a handful of group members (or their covered dependents) may submit claims, the expectation is that the majority will not. The premiums paid by that majority over many years will make it worthwhile for the insurer to insure a group—sight unseen. So the short answer is that medical testing is waived as long as the insurer feels comfortable that the group is sufficiently diverse in terms of age and state of health.

If you own your practice and it's large enough to qualify for group insurance plans, you should be eligible for those group offerings as an employee of your firm, and you may elect to supplement them with private policies.

Group Health Insurance

Recent legislation has changed the group health care responsibilities of small business owners. Make sure you fully understand your firm's obligations, which will depend primarily on its size in terms of eligible employees. Seek the advice of a professional health insurance professional and compare multiple plans to identify one that works best for you and your staff. If your practice is very large, you may be obligated to provide an in-house health plan. If your firm is smaller, you may be able to provide money to employees to purchase a plan from one of the newly formed health care plan exchanges. Discuss this with your health insurance representative.

Group Umbrella Insurance

As discussed in Book I, umbrella insurance is a cheap and effective way to raise your family's personal liability limits. The typical homeowner's and auto insurance policies provide liability coverage up to $300,000 or $500,000. A single serious car accident can create liabilities well over these limits, which could mean that your family's pillars would have to be liquidated and the proceeds given to victims or their families. Umbrella insurance may easily and affordably raise your coverage limit to several million dollars, protecting you against such risk exposure.

According to Andrew F. Howard, President and CEO of Howard Insurance, there are *group personal umbrella* insurance policies that can be procured by a business. These programs may give eligible employees access to higher personal liability limits with less underwriting (simpler approval process), at a lower cost than they would pay on their own. Such policies can be an affordable way to reward employees and enhance loyalty to the practice. As a qualifying employee of the practice, you can be personally eligible for this benefit.

Group Life Insurance

Group life insurance can be made available to employees, providing their families or other designated beneficiaries with a lump sum payment in the event of the covered employee's death. Group life insurance policies often specify the amount of coverage as a multiple of the employee's most recent annual salary. Typical multipliers range from one to three years. In the grand scheme of things, that is, when one takes into account outstanding mortgage payments and children's anticipated college costs, group life policies tend to provide helpful but insufficient coverage. Accordingly, many doctors supplement group life policies with private policies (discussed in Book I).

Group Disability Insurance

Group disability insurance can be made available to staff as a mechanism for protecting their incomes in the event of debilitating illness or injury. In the event a covered employee becomes disabled, basic group disability policies will pay the employee directly, for the duration of the benefit period. If you (the owner) sign up for the group policy as an employee of your practice and subsequently become disabled, you should also be eligible for benefits.

If you receive disability benefits from a policy that was paid for by your employer (the medical practice), you may be responsible for paying taxes on those benefits.

Medical professionals' incomes tend to be higher than the population average, which often means that the limits of coverage on basic group policies fall short of their needs. For this reason, many doctors supplement group insurance with their own private sources of disability insurance (discussed in Book I).

Business Insurance

We now review those insurance products that are uniquely suited to addressing business risks.

General Liability Insurance

In the same way that you may be personally liable for injuries suffered by others on your personal property (or caused by you or your car), your practice (as a distinct legal entity) may be liable for damages or injuries to others. It's important to note that personal insurance policies (in particular liability insurance under homeowner's or auto policies) often don't cover losses or damage incurred while you are on the job—and *vice versa* (business policies may not cover personal exposures). The upshot is that you should have distinct personal and business insurance policies in place and that each of them must provide sufficient coverage. This is a reminder that you should discuss your needs carefully with a qualified insurance agent.

Make sure all your facilities and staff are properly covered including any vehicles used for business purposes. The limits of liability should be examined closely to ensure sufficiency in the event a serious injury occurs. The practice (or you) may be personally liable for any excess liability above and beyond a policy's stated limits.

Professional Malpractice Insurance

Medical malpractice insurance is discussed in some detail in Book I. While some of that material is repeated here, you may wish to review Book I's Employment Contract and Estate Planning chapters.

Medical malpractice insurance (Med Mal) exists to cover your practice's attorney fees and any judgments against your practice or staff members (or you personally).

The employment contract used with your staff members should specify any medical malpractice insurance provided and the terms of that insurance. Since premiums for such insurance can be high, and claims can be overwhelming, Med Mal is an important consideration in such contracts both for the employee and for you as owner.

A crucial consideration when purchasing Med Mal insurance is whether the policies are based on *occurrence* or *claims-made*. With Claims Made policies there will likely be a need to purchase *Tail* coverage for any departing medical professional. At the time of hiring, it should be made clear who will be responsible for purchasing that Tail, which can cost as much as 2.5 times the previous annual premium.

Under malpractice insurance policies, the insurer will usually pay for legal defense. Unlike most other insurance types, there is usually no deductible requirement in Med Mal policies.

Statutes of limitations on actions taken on medical malpractice grounds can vary widely. On the high end they can be up to 21 years for pediatricians (limitation for them is 3 years after the minor becomes an adult). Needless to say, with such a lengthy span of time over which liability persists, it's necessary to ensure you have the tail protection in place!

There are limits specified in Med Mal policies. The insurer is only responsible for payments up to these limits. Any additional awards above and beyond must be made up from the assets of the practice or from the individual physicians' personal assets (including your own). This can be very damaging. Entire practices have been wiped out by liability awards in excess of insurance. It behooves you to know how much coverage your policy provides to your practice, and for you to gauge whether that is likely to protect you sufficiently. Ignoring these issues can mean putting some of your pillars of wealth in danger.

The *New England Journal of Medicine* has addressed the topic in a (2011) article: "Malpractice Risk According to Physician Specialty." There is also information available on the Practice Management section of the American College of Physicians website.

The American Medical Association is another potential resource for information on professional legal liability. It publishes the book *Physician Professional Liability Market and Regulatory Environment*.

Key Person Insurance

Suppose you start a medical practice and realize after some time that you are heavily reliant on an outstanding administrator (one of those we sometimes refer to as *worth her weight in gold*). You know that the practice would suffer greatly in the event she became disabled or deceased. So you purchase *key person insurance* which pays the business in the event either tragedy occurs. That payment allows you to immediately hire a highly qualified temporary administrator and/or to pay an executive search firm to find a permanent replacement. This helps to ensure business continuity.

Business Overhead Expense

In the event an owner becomes disabled, *Business Overhead Expense* insurance reimburses the business for normal operating expenses. Eligible expenses usually include rent, employee salaries, payroll taxes, utilities, property taxes, insurance, etc. The point of this insurance is to give a disabled business owner one to two years in which to decide what to do with the business: sell it, close it, or bring a new partner in to take over management.

Business Loan Coverage

In the event of a disability, *Business Loan Coverage* insurance pays the principal and interest on eligible outstanding business loans. Qualifying loans often include those used to buy equipment, an existing business, or the real estate on which the business is located.

This can be particularly important as the lender may be entitled to "call-in" (demand early payment on the entire loan outstanding) if some "material" (significant) event has occurred. The disability of the principal earner in a business is significant and may allow the bank to call the loan and ultimately even seize assets which may have been pledged as collateral on the loan. Having business loan coverage insurance in place is an effective way to thwart such a move, as the lender will likely be content to receive the ongoing payments from the insurer instead of trying to call the loan early.

Student Loans

Some insurers will provide coverage on student loans issued to medical, dental, law, veterinary or pharmacy students. There is usually a ceiling on the amount covered under these insurance products. $2,000 per month is a typical maximum. In the event of disability, the insurer will pay up to $2,000 per month directly to the lender. This can make a big difference to your monthly finances if you are carrying large amounts of school debt.

Disability Buy-Out

Disability Buy-Out insurance applies to businesses with two or more owners (and usually up to about eight or ten owners). The policy is designed to provide a significant enough amount for the other (non-disabled) owners/partners to buy out the disabled owner/partner. Benefits may be paid in monthly installments or as a lump sum.

This mechanism provides a win-win for everyone: the disabled individual and her family can receive money to help them cope with the disability, and the business can continue without being burdened by an owner who can no longer contribute.

Hire Staff

Several months prior to opening for business, you should be interviewing prospective employees. You will likely need to fill some combination of the following positions:

1. An office manager/administrator
2. Receptionist
3. Billing specialist
4. Nurse(s)/Dental hygienist(s)/Physician assistant(s)
5. Other physicians or dentists with appropriate specialties

In a very small practice (at least early on), you may find that one capable person, along with yourself, can combine to cover all required roles. Occasionally, the doctor's spouse may take on some of these duties, in particular office manager or administrator roles, and potentially receptionist, billing specialist, and even nurse or dental hygienist (assuming the spouse is qualified and licensed to undertake such duties).

Your business plan should identify all required positions, a timeline specifying when each role will be added, as well as the total cost of having each employee on the payroll. Those costs include salary, but also other associated costs. When budgeting for a full time position, you may wish to multiply the full time salary (including bonus) by 1.3, where the additional 30% is intended to capture additional costs including taxes and benefits. Your accountant should be able to tell you whether a different multiplier is appropriate.

You should also budget for the hiring process. It takes time and money to post help-wanted ads, to sift through submitted resumes, and then to interview and follow up with leading candidates. There are also legal costs to finalize contracts and employment agreements.

The irony is that early on you may want to do as much of the legal contracting work yourself in order to save money. But early on, when you are least experienced, is exactly when you need the most help from experienced attorneys. The best advice is: pay the professionals to make sure your contracts are solid.

You'll want to ensure that all staff members are qualified and properly credentialed. Check appropriate databases to ensure their qualifications are in good standing. If you like a person who lacks some credentials, you can make hiring contingent on completion of necessary training and certification.

Background checks are advisable to ensure staff are properly qualified and screened, but full background checks can be expensive, so you need to balance the *need to know* with the *cost to know*.

Keep in mind that you'll be working with these people every day for years. You want them to be capable, reliable and easy to get along with. Yes, you can always fire and replace staff, but such a cavalier attitude assumes that the process of replacement is easy and cheap. It is neither. So don't hire the first person through the door. Yes, it's tempting to make hiring decisions quickly and believe you can move on to other priorities, but having to fire and recruit others is nerve-wrenching and time consuming. It's far more efficient to spend time upfront finding the right person, than it is to make hasty choices which must be reversed a few months later.

Provision of medical services is a deeply personal and intimate job that calls for skilled and caring people. If you don't pay your best employees well enough to keep them, you will lose them to another employer—possibly even to a direct competitor.

High staff turnover is a bad sign at any company. It will be noticed by your patients, and it can also hurt you in terms of higher worker's compensation costs and recruiting and training costs. Finally, there is the very real cost to you of being distracted from serving your patients each time you have to interview and negotiate with new employees.

Additional guidance on hiring, assessing, and terminating staff is provided in Part II of this book, in the managing human resources chapter.

Order Equipment and Supplies

To deliver services you will need specialized equipment, furniture, and supplies. A dentist will need hi-tech chairs, a psychiatrist will need appropriate furnishings to put patients at ease, a cardiologist may need a treadmill and EKG machine, and an orthopedic surgeon may need an X-ray machine.

Some of the equipment will be highly sophisticated and precisely engineered: in other words—expensive! In fact, some equipment is so expensive that you will have to lease it instead of buying it. Your business plan should list all required equipment along with prices and expected maintenance costs. You will then need to coordinate receipt of the equipment such that it arrives in time to be properly installed and used. Equipment which arrives too late will deprive you of much needed revenue. Equipment that arrives too early also poses a problem. It has to sit around in the midst of the build-out, where it may be damaged.

Select equipment vendors who are reliable and provide timely service. Every minute a machine is down for maintenance means the practice is losing money.

In addition to equipment and furnishings, your practice will require supplies, such as hospital gowns, syringes, bandages, cotton balls, swabs, paper cups, etc. An electronic inventory system will help you track supplies, ensuring that you are holding just the right amount of each item.

Ordering too many items in advance creates several problems: One, more cash gets tied up in inventory instead of being available for other needs. Two, you have to find storage space for all that inventory, taking up space that could be used more effectively. For example, reducing inventory may enable you to repurpose a storage room into a new treatment room, allowing you to see more patients each day, thereby increasing profitability.

Not ordering enough supplies also presents problems: mainly, while awaiting replenishments you won't be able to offer some of your services, which could mean losing potential revenue.

As part of your business plan, identify the suppliers you intend to use and confirm that they are ready and willing to work with you, under conditions that are acceptable to you. For example, they will be able to ship supplies on short notice and with quick delivery times.

Dealing with a single supplier may seem more convenient, but what happens if that single provider lets you down? In the risk management chapter we'll discuss the importance of having relationships with several suppliers.

Oversee Design and Build-out

By all accounts, the build-out is one of the most frustrating elements of opening a medical practice. There are many reasons for this, including poor planning, ambiguous contract language, misunderstandings, shoddy work, and approval delays by local government agencies.

Some of these frustrations may be avoided by working with a skilled architect, who can be very helpful in the early design and build-out stages (subject to budgetary constraints). An architect is a must if you are considering new construction or significant modification of existing space. The architect may be hired directly by you (the doctor), by the landlord, or by a contractor.

It's generally a good idea to engage the architect early in the process, allowing her to provide opinions on location choices and how easily each can be adapted to your needs. Questions that should be addressed include: where do you want the treatment rooms and where would you like to have the doctors' offices? Which rooms (examination rooms, storage rooms, or offices) should be adjacent? What arrangement will yield the best flow and function? In addition, engaging the architect early in the process may allow you to more accurately predict gross overall costs, which in turn enables a more realistic conversation with lenders about financing.

A very large project may require much earlier involvement by the architect. A year in advance is generally appropriate for small practices.

You may not need an architect at all if you are taking over space from another doctor and the landlord offers to re-carpet and re-paint, leaving only minor tweaking for you to complete. A minor item includes cutting out a window or moving a door on a non-supporting wall.

If you're taking an entire floor, and you know the space is flexible enough to meet your needs, you may not need the architect upfront, but you should consider engaging an architect after the lease is finalized to begin the floor planning process.

Some specialized contractors can provide a professional build-out and documentation for permitting, but they may miss building code issues or they may not pay sufficient attention to space design requirements. The classic example is that of a contractor's plans for an orthopedist's reception room, which called for putting two chairs at 90 degrees in the reception room. This arrangement completely neglected space for people's legs—a problem in any reception area but especially in this case, because many patients came in with leg braces and couldn't bend at the knee.

Architects tend not to make these kinds of mistakes. They will also tell you that unlike contractors, they tend to have a more aesthetic design sense, which forms a big part of their training.

It's prudent to have a commercial real estate lawyer review architect and contractor contracts whenever you contract directly with either of them. When the landlord contracts directly with the architect and contractors, the landlord's attorney will be involved.

If you're viewing shell space (skeleton space without walls or floors) the landowner will typically be contracting directly with the architect and contractor. Your attorney should, of course, be involved in the lease signing with the landlord.

The Build-out Process

According to architect Ken Lewis, the build-out process generally begins with the architect formulating several documents:

Program Document: The *Program Document* outlines basics such as the number of rooms intended, the size of each room, and the major amenities or facilities required in each room.

Space Plan Document: A *Space Plan* shows the various rooms and general dimensions.

You should take the time to provide feedback to the architect on these two documents. All-too-often, lack of focus and limited engagement by doctors lead to delays. In many cases this is because the doctor is juggling full-time work while planning his new private practice. In some cases the doctor just finds the material boring and can't get motivated to read and respond.

The next step once these documents have been drafted is to begin considering the finishing touches: choices of lighting, carpet, paint, etc. Material costs come into play as well and this is where it's crucially important for you to have a vision of what the space is meant to achieve and its intended atmosphere. The standard recommendation is to begin with a wish-list or ideal build-out scenario. Then you can price that out and compare to existing space and financing constraints. Often this means that some features need to be rethought and perhaps replaced with cheaper alternatives or left out entirely. Sometimes certain features turn out to be less expensive than originally forecast, and they can be added without breaking the bank. Doing this analysis upfront helps to get everyone's expectations aligned with reality.

Doctors tend to think everything is overly expensive. This may be due to lack of experience with commercial spaces, or too much experience with retail (home) situations. As Ken Lewis points out, commercial spaces are different and tend to be more expensive.

Sometimes the medical specialty influences the doctor's perspective on costs and budgets. For example, internal medicine practices tend to have lower margins (profitability) and make money off volume, while radiology is a higher margin business with a focus on testing. Accordingly, the default perspective for an internal medicine specialist may reflect greater aversion to spending. In contrast, a radiologist may fully expect that equipment procurement will be expensive and therefore that budgets will have to be larger.

Architects are sometimes frustrated because it can take a long time to fully engage the doctor, to obtain feedback on preliminary documents, to update expectations and to arrange financing. Delays in these early phases necessarily compress all other deadlines. This makes it harder for everyone, including the architect, to do what needs to be done in the time remaining.

You should negotiate hard with all counterparties, including the architect and contractors, but do so for the right reasons and in professional fashion. Some doctors negotiate hard purely due to ego or because they are afraid of getting ripped off, even though they have been offered a fair deal. Yet others don't want to be involved and hand off all negotiations to their accountant or attorney. As noted earlier, this can get expensive.

Design Development Document: The next document that may be needed is the *Design Development Document.* It includes some information on interior elevations, ceiling plans, and may show cabinetry and other room-specific details.

Final Construction Document: The *Final Construction Document* contains all technical details and is used to interact with engineer(s), to finalize pricing with contractors, and to secure required permits from local authorities.

Words of Caution

As noted elsewhere in this book, some doctors fail to produce a coherent business plan and neglect to formulate a value proposition and strategic goals. In the absence of these guideposts, efforts to open a facility often wither. The typical story begins with a doctor who expends (wastes) a lot of time unsuccessfully seeking financing (banks don't like to give money to people who lack focus and managerial skills). The story proceeds with an inability to secure staff (candidates are discouraged by lack of planning). And it's all downhill from there. The project unravels and dies. Beyond the time expended on a fruitless endeavor, the doctor has usually also incurred some cost—with nothing to show for it. The key to avoiding this mistake is to plan ahead!

Another common challenge is that when projects do get underway and development progresses, doctors don't always understand what they are really getting. This is often because they don't take any interest in the aforementioned documents. In fairness, not everyone relates well to a 2-dimensional floor plan. But in other cases it's attributable to doctors' attitudes—they simply don't think the documents are important. (It's possible to create 3-dimensional models but that costs more and often doesn't add value).

The bottom line is that failure to take an active interest in the documents leads to misunderstandings. When expectations are not aligned because the floor plan is misunderstood by the doctor, expensive changes may have to be made later in the process. Not to mention the finger-pointing and recriminations that sour relationships and productivity. It's far better to plan carefully in advance rather than having to make changes when the project is in full swing.

Once the architect's plans are ready, the next stage of the process is to obtain bids from multiple contractors and to select among them. The work cannot begin until contracts are signed. Once the ink dries on the contracts, the contractor should submit the plans to the local jurisdiction (county or city government) for permits. Your team has no control over the amount of time local government officials spend reviewing your documents. Delays at this stage can be unpredictable, lengthy, frustrating, and can play havoc with the rest of your timeline.

As completion of the various preliminary build-out steps drags on, the actual construction window becomes compressed. The alternative is to delay the practice's opening date, which can be both financially and emotionally draining.

The obvious remedy is to allow enough time for all of these steps, and to be proactive in responding to the architect and other professionals along the way. When it comes to opening a practice, one cannot snap one's fingers and have everything completed magically. It is a process and each phase must be completed in turn.

Ken Lewis points out that there is a key milestone known as achieving *Substantial Completion*. This means the contractor has substantially completed 99% of the necessary work and it's possible to obtain an occupancy permit. A *Punch List* (a list of identified deficiencies) of typically minor outstanding work items is drawn up. Items on the list may include touching up some paint, gluing down loose wallpaper, replacing a damaged door handle, etc. These are the final items that need to be completed prior to move in.

When the timeline becomes compressed for the reasons stated above, doctor(s) may rush to move into an incomplete space. This creates a situation in which construction work progresses in the midst of an active medical practice, making it difficult for the architect and doctor to do a detailed walk-through and document outstanding deficiencies. It also sets the stage for other problems. Here's one example of a dentist who began to position equipment in rooms that were not yet completed. The next day some broken drywall was discovered which was not on the Punch list. The contractor contended that the movers acting on the dentist's behalf broke the wall, while the dentist insisted the break was there earlier, should have been on the Punch List, and was the contractor's responsibility. The actual fix was neither expensive nor time consuming, but the episode contributed to discord between the contractor's workers and the practice's employees.

Any deviations from the original agreement signed with the contractor require *Change Orders*. Most Change Orders are associated with higher costs, but some can be used to reduce costs. For example, you originally wanted expensive tiles, but subsequently decide lower-cost carpet will be better (you can realize the savings as long as none of the expensive tiling material has already been ordered). Usually, however, the *Contract Number* (the contractually agreed-upon total dollar amount payable for construction) goes up— not down.

There are broadly 3 types of Change Orders:

1. The doctor decides to change something. It's clear that the doctor will be responsible for paying for the change(s).
2. Unanticipated or hidden conditions are discovered which require additional work. For example, a plan calls for adding a sink along an existing wall. When the contractor opens the wall up it is discovered to be full of mold. No one knew it was there but someone (doctor or landlord) has to pay for remediation. An alternative example is when the permit provider (city or county) demands unanticipated changes. Under either of these scenarios it can be challenging to determine which party is responsible for shouldering the costs.
3. An item has been omitted from the plan. For example, the planning documents fail to show a countertop and the contractor hasn't included it in the price. In this case, the doctor still needs to pay for it because it's clearly needed as part of the basic setup and the doctor will benefit from obtaining it.

Because Change Orders often mean a more expensive build-out, it's advisable that you build a *Contingency* into your original loan request. For example, ask for a $525,000 loan from the bank instead of $500,000. This reflects some buffer above and beyond the initially established amounts. It's easier to do this upfront rather than having to negotiate an increase with the lender after the fact.

Legal language specifying when lease payments are due to begin is crucial. You don't want to be on the hook for lease payments before the facility is substantially completed and available for you to begin generating revenue. A savvy commercial real estate attorney will know to look for these contract terms, which often refer to the *Lease Commencement Date*. A fair contract will begin lease payments upon Substantial Completion at which time you are able to obtain the occupancy permit and the premises can be turned over for use— which means you can generate income! The Lease Commencement Date also begins the clock ticking on the traditional one-year warranty provided by the contractor, during which the contractor is still responsible for construction issues, for example, a leaking valve or loose flooring.

Finally, keep in mind that the legal standard of care by participating parties is *not* to produce perfect documents. The implication is that during the process you may not be looking at perfect plans and may not be able to demand perfect ones. Everyone involved (architect, contractor, landowner) should have insurance to cover gray areas.

The Contractor's Perspective

The most frustrating element of the build-out phase tends to be the interaction with contractors. These are the people who actually do the work: they pull out the old carpet, revamp the plumbing, change the ceiling tiles, paint the walls, move doorways, rewire electrical systems, etc.

Many contractors are highly specialized. That is, they may only do plumbing, or electrical work, or fire control and suppression systems. This means you may find yourself having to manage multiple contractor teams, each responsible for a different task, some of which may have to be completed in a specific order. It can be costly to discover that one contractor has already covered all the walls with wallpaper but the electrician has yet to complete all the rewiring in the walls. Or that the expensive tiles have been laid on the floor but the plumbing team still needs to rip up parts of the floor to lay new pipes.

Ben Bashiri, a contractor specializing in medical spaces, cautions doctors not to use too many providers. A single turnkey solution is simpler, less time consuming and fully coordinated by experienced professionals. If you choose not to go with the turnkey solution, you must coordinate separately with the: mechanical, electrical and plumbing (MEP) engineer(s), developer, architect, contractor(s), interior designer, etc. This is especially challenging for smaller practices, where it isn't worth it for the doctor to deal with each contractor directly.

A crucial element of any contract work is that the completed space must be compliant with safety regulations. You can't open your doors to the public (to patients) until you have proper certifications from the fire inspector and the local (city or county) government. A good contractor will be well connected with relevant local government entities and will automatically help you with filing of appropriate paperwork, application for occupancy and other required permits.

Echoing concerns expressed by many other professionals involved in the process, Ben Bashiri states that doctors often don't allow enough time for decision making. He suggests that they need to budget more time for their own research on location, design, and materials. Failure to plan ahead leads to misunderstandings, distrust and finger-pointing. Most importantly, it wastes time and money.

The bottom line is that there's no alternative to putting in the time, and it needs to be quality time where the doctor's attention is fully focused on plan details. Bashiri's rule is that he will meet with clients at any time (including after regular business hours) but the clients must leave their cell phones and pagers behind. This ensures that everyone's attention is properly focused, decisions can be made quickly and effectively, and there are no painful misunderstandings and recriminations.

Another reason to meet and discuss all details in advance is that doctors often don't understand why materials and furnishings cost so much. There are several reasons: The medical industry is very abusive to furnishings and equipment. A regular cabinet in a private home may be opened 6 times a day, but a sterilization cabinet in a medical office may be opened 50-100 times daily. It's therefore necessary to use the correct materials, despite their higher price initially. There is a real gain to using materials which can cut down on maintenance and cleaning. For example, a surface that is easier to clean and disinfect can cut several minutes off the cleaning routine per dental patient. Over a full day that can make a meaningful difference in the number of patients examined or the number of staff employed. Those who cut costs on materials are hurting themselves in the long run. In an efficient practice every second and every minute counts.

Equipment has also become very expensive due to increasingly demanding environmental safety requirements as well as noise abatement requirements (which may be imposed by landlords who want to ensure there isn't significant noise emanating from a practice and disturbing other residents).

Doctors are often unaware that there's lots of free consulting available to them from real estate agents, developers, and contractors. Consequently, few doctors take advantage of these resources and end up coming short on advanced planning.

Market the Practice

Marketing is often the most neglected element in a medical practice, for several reasons:

1. Few people are comfortable "selling themselves". Many of us are brought up to believe that singing our own praises or announcing all the wonderful things we can do is akin to "showing off."
2. Marketing requires time—a commodity medical practitioners never have in sufficient supply. Treating a patient takes higher priority than writing an article for the practice's newsletter or proofreading material for the practice's website.
3. Some of us simply aren't interested in the marketing process. It's tough to give priority to activities we find boring.

The unavoidable fact is that *all* businesses need some marketing, and some businesses are entirely dependent on effective marketing. Quite simply, you can't ignore marketing. You must budget reasonably for marketing expenses and you must do what is necessary until you are satisfied that your marketing dollars are achieving the desired impact. If they are not, you need to make changes until you reach the desired level of effectiveness.

Marketing is not a one-time effort. It's a process: one which depends heavily on feedback and continuous adjustments.

Allen Schiff suggests that a start-up dental practice should budget approximately $40,000 for marketing. Subsequently, marketing expenditures should be around 3-4% of total collected fees (total revenue) per year. A mature dental practice should be spending 2-3% of total collected fees per year. Samuel Luxenburg recommends spending around 6% of total revenue on marketing, with about half that amount spent on existing patients and half directed at prospective clients. The specific nature and location of each practice (whether dental or medical) must be taken into account when budgeting for marketing expenditures.

Why does a mature practice require ongoing marketing? After all, once you have a loyal customer base that is happy to refer friends and family to you, why is any marketing expenditure needed? The simple answer is that even the most successful practices experience natural *attrition* (loss of clients). There are many reasons for attrition: patients move away, they become "cured", their in-law offers to treat them at a deep discount, or they dislike some aspect of your service. Even mature and successful practices can expect double digit attrition annually. That is, loss of more than 10% of patients per year. According to an American Dental Association Marketing Study, attrition at mature dental practices ranges from 12% to 16% annually. The implication is that if you are not marketing on an ongoing basis, you are falling behind. You must engage in marketing just to maintain a certain client population size. If you want to grow, you need to increase marketing efforts even further.

You can experiment using flyers, mailings, the Internet and social media. Special deals can sometimes be used to draw new prospective patients to your practice. This tends to be more relevant for retail oriented practices (for example, an ophthalmologist can offer specials on a second pair of glasses or contacts, or a dentist can offer special cleaning rates for children).

In the Internet Age, traditional print advertizing has become less relevant. Make sure your marketing dollars are spent most effectively. Whenever a campaign doesn't seem to be effective—seek to understand why, and then make changes.

It's a good idea to seek testimonials from happy customers and use them appropriately to establish credibility. Ask enthusiastic patients to provide favorable reviews on Angie's List and any other relevant sites.

You can also consider offering bonuses to employees who bring in new patients. In some industries there are limitations on who can receive financial compensation for bringing in patients/clients or on the amount of compensation that is allowed. Make sure your arrangements are consistent with laws and regulations.

Make it easy for patients to contact the practice and to set or change appointments. Set up a user-friendly website, and consider using an electronic appointment system that gives patients more control and convenience.

Remind all staff members that each of them is an ambassador of the firm. Each of them can contribute to making the practice more successful—or less successful. Their attitude, empathy, sincerity, helpfulness and expertise all matter.

It can be a good idea to engage the services of a specialized marketing consultant. The best ones will have direct experience working within your medical specialty area, and an understanding of local conditions.

Don't underestimate the usefulness of networking with local professionals who may agree to refer patients to you—often with the expectation that you will do the same for them. The best arrangements are reciprocal. If a general doctor refers lots of patients to you and receives nothing in return, she may well decide to start referring to one of your competitors instead.

Furthermore, remember that every time someone refers to you, the originating doctor takes on some reputation risk. For example, if the referred patient ends up having a bad experience with you, he may take that frustration out on the physician who recommended you—and will likely never recommend you again. So, view each referral with the respect it deserves.

As already noted, marketing is an ongoing process. It doesn't stop when the doors first open for business. In fact, once the patients begin to come in, you can and should seek information from them that helps to refine your marketing messages. Ask how patients found out about your practice and why they chose to visit you. Think about common characteristics among those who are inclined to become your patients. Do they represent a particular age group, cultural background, gender, etc.? Seek to understand the patterns. It's possible that your practice has some comparative advantage and if so, it's important to identify that advantage and use it. Once you begin to ask these questions routinely, you'll have an ongoing source of feedback to help adjust the way your business is conducted, with a view to optimizing the client experience. Ultimately, your best marketing comes from satisfied customers.

Public Presentations

It's likely that some of your marketing will involve public presentations delivered by you or your colleagues.

In a medical school, internship, or fellowship setting the only thing that matters is the intellectual rigor of your arguments. In a business setting everything else suddenly matters. This includes your physical appearance and clothing, the aesthetic appeal of your presentation materials, as well as your confidence and vocal intonation. While these may seem frivolous to those who care about science and medicine, they cannot be ignored in a business setting.

Objectively assess your own public speaking abilities. You can join a variety of professional groups that provide an opportunity for you to speak publicly and receive constructive feedback. The *Pillars of Wealth* initiative (pillarsofwealth.com) provides such opportunities through the formation of local professional groups where medical practitioners can meet periodically to discuss best practices, industry trends, concerns, implications of new legislation, and to market their practices and specialties. Groups are generally designed to include a maximum of one practitioner from each specialty area. This avoids competitive strains and allows all participants to contribute and explore: opportunities for reciprocal client referrals, sharing of staff, initiatives to jointly market and/or reduce overhead, etc. Feel free to contact us at pillarsofwealth.com to explore formation of a group in your area.

Commercial Orientation

Another element of your marketing plan should be to instill a commercial orientation in everyone associated with the practice. This means that every person in the firm, regardless of role, understands that he is part of a business and is sufficiently professional to do his part, especially when facing patients. Commercial orientation means that a receptionist behaves professionally when a patient is accidentally transferred on a phone line, and a janitor knows it's important to politely redirect a patient who is wandering aimlessly in the hallways.

In contrast, when a commercial orientation is absent, people (and subsequently practices) tend to under-perform. The receptionist hangs up on patients, the janitor ignores lost visitors, and doctors forget patients in waiting rooms.

As noted earlier, everyone is (at all times) an ambassador of the firm to the outside world. Everyone markets, everyone advertises, everyone identifies process errors, everyone pays attention to patient needs. Practices that achieve this level of focus and professionalism do much better than those that do not.

Identify your star performers—those who excel at client service and practice proper ambassadorship, and have them train their colleagues. If such people are not present in the firm, add "commercial orientation" to your list of required skills for new hires.

Remember at all times that you are the "ambassador-in-chief." Lead by example to emphasize to all staff members that the highest level of client service is expected and demanded.

Train the Staff

The health care industry requires very specific skills and is highly regulated. This means there are many potential risks for you as an owner in the event an employee performs poorly. Accordingly, it's crucial to ensure staff members are prepared to do their jobs and do them well—before the first patient walks in the door. Staff must be trained and properly qualified for use of equipment and technology solutions. Everyone must also hold all relevant licenses.

If activities in your practice are fairly straightforward, it may be easy to bring in new staff members and have them ready for action within a matter of weeks. On the other hand, if your activities will require very precise and unique expertise you may need to plan for several months of education and rehearsal.

Some procedures require handling of highly specialized equipment or medication. Vendors of these products often offer training, but their training schedules may be somewhat inflexible. Find out in advance what those schedules are and make sure you leave enough time for training (and licensing) to take place prior to opening doors for business.

Training is an ongoing activity. Many staff members will be required to complete continuing education courses throughout their careers.

Open for Business

Not so fast! It's not quite as simple as hanging an 'OPEN' sign on your door one fine morning.

To have a successful opening day you must complete all the steps outlined in Part I of this book—and then some. Proper groundwork has to be laid before patients begin to walk in off the street, respond to your advertisements, or become referred to you by other professionals.

Generally, there are two launch types: hard and soft. A *hard* launch is proverbially accompanied by blaring trumpets and flesh-pressing politicians. This hard launch occurs on a specific date and within the context of a well-orchestrated event, pre-advertized in the media. It is a formal opening designed to make a loud splash and attract as much attention as possible.

A soft launch, as the name implies, is an informal opening: one that is not heavily advertized. It often makes sense to have both a soft and a hard launch. The soft launch provides an opportunity to begin getting the word out regarding your practice in low-key and low-pressure fashion. During the soft launch you may be open for a limited number of hours, allowing you an opportunity to service a small number of patients in a careful and measured way. This enables you to test out all processes, systems, and equipment. It also serves as a "dress-rehearsal" of sorts for the staff.

A major advantage of the soft launch is that it allows you to kick the tires on your own business and refine and correct your processes to ensure they adhere to your Value Proposition and Mission

Statement. And if something goes wrong, you can avoid suffering heavy reputational damage.

Later, as the kinks in your processes and personnel preparation are ironed out, you can increase hours of operation and the overall intensity of business activities.

Your rent will likely begin to come due once you begin seeing patients, so choose the soft launch date carefully and be prepared to ramp up quickly thereafter.

PART II: RUNNING THE PRACTICE

Running your practice on an ongoing basis is a natural extension of launching it, but there is a different focus. The emphasis shifts from figuring everything out for the first time and improvising solutions to managing processes and maximizing efficiencies.

The focus on management and efficiency is the subject of Part II of this book, which proceeds with chapters on:

- Leading and managing
- Managing human resources
- Financial management
- Legal and regulatory considerations
- Best practices
- Risk management
- Words of wisdom from other private practitioners

Appendix 1 addresses some of the main considerations for those seeking to purchase an existing practice.

Leading and Managing

As a business owner you must lead and manage the practice on an ongoing basis. "Leadership" and "management," or "leader" and "manager," are often used interchangeably, but they refer to different skill sets:

- *Leadership* has to do with the ability to inspire others and gain their trust; to convey a strategic vision other people will voluntarily support. Leadership is about changing mindsets, convincing people of the need to effect change, establishing why your vision is correct, or why it may be more correct than the current path

- *Management* refers to the ability to direct people to combine their diverse experiences and talents in the most effective way to produce desired results. It requires emotional competencies to identify abilities and skill deficiencies in others, and the analytical ability to determine how to combine people within a team to optimize performance

Leadership is more inspirational in nature; management's focus is more operational.

Countless books have been written on the subjects of management and leadership, including deep explorations of the differences between them. The abbreviated definitions provided above suffice for our purposes.

The distinctions are necessary because you may have a natural inclination to one or the other of these skill sets, but not both. Take heart: relatively few people are naturally inclined to both skill sets, and development of each requires training and experience. That is, leaders (and managers) are not born—they are made.

Accordingly, your personal affinity for leadership or management (or neither) should not be interpreted as good or bad, it is simply something to be aware of. Once you attain this awareness, add people to your team who offer those skills or inclinations you do not possess.

In seeking to attain this self awareness, the relatively easy part is to decide which activities you personally like or dislike. The potentially tricky part is admitting to yourself that you may not be particularly good at one or the other (or both). These considerations must not be driven by ego, but rather by simple logic: if you insist on monopolizing duties that others can perform better you will harm your practice. Alternatively, by handing select duties off to others, everyone can focus on doing what they do best, which invariably helps the practice to prosper. Another way to put this is: do you prefer to call all the shots and be the owner of a struggling practice, or are you comfortable sharing some duties and being the proud owner of a thriving practice?

A common arrangement is one in which you, the owner, function as the leader of the medical or dental practice, providing the vision and inspiring others to join you in creating services that meet patient needs. Alongside you presides an administrator who competently manages the practice such that it delivers in a practical way on your vision's promise.

In the following chapters we discuss various skills, competencies, processes, and activities required for success. When discussing skills, for the sake of brevity, we will not constantly seek to classify them as leadership or management skills. It is useful for you, however, to be aware of the distinctions as you shepherd your practice along over time.

Managing Human Resources

Hang on a minute! Haven't we already talked about hiring and training staff? Why are we talking about human resources again?

The answer is that management of human resources may well be your biggest challenge, and you must deal with it properly. Few factors are as important to a successful practice as its people. One of the most common statements by CEOs is that "people are our greatest asset." While this is sometimes an insincere statement made for political consumption, it is a fact, and especially within a medical practice context, where it is a mantra.

Patients seek medical attention when they are ill, injured, and/or unhappy. In other words, they are often at their worst: depressed, self conscious, and fearful. The fastest path to success is to provide them with an environment that is supportive and empathetic. Contrary to common belief, such an atmosphere is not created by lavish waterfalls in the reception area, or fancy coffee service. Rather, it is created and nurtured by sincere people whose empathy comes across naturally.

However brilliant you may be as a provider of medical services, most of your patients will form their lasting opinions based on the human elements of their experience at your practice: sincerity, empathy, and a sense of human connection.

With all this in mind, it should be clear that managing your human resources is a key ingredient to success. Without it, you will most likely fail or at the very least, severely hamper financial performance.

The real world business environment is different from the academic one to which medical practitioners are exposed as students. Consider a university laboratory setting headed by a physician or dentist. Staff often consists of dental or medical students, and other graduate students (Masters and Ph.D.s in the life sciences). All of these people are deeply connected to the laboratory, which is often headed by their thesis advisor or the person who will write their recommendation letters to medical or dental schools. When human conflicts arise in these settings (conflicts arise in any setting), the medical practitioner in charge can often ignore them, because the graduate students must settle their differences one way or another— they can't just move elsewhere as this could jeopardize their entire career. The upshot is that the doctor in charge can often disregard these human resource-related issues and simply tell everyone involved to focus and get on with their duties.

In the "real" world, human conflicts must be managed more proactively. Otherwise, people will simply leave. The cost of replacing staff can be very high, especially when they have crucial institutional knowledge. For example, if they are the only people who know how to make the billing system work or the only ones who know how to satisfy regulators over compliance issues.

Private practice is a business, and a business and its people must be managed carefully. Authoritarian systems don't succeed in a free market and free labor environment. In a competitive economy you must pay good people well if you wish to keep them. According to Sage Growth Partners CEO Don McDaniel, some doctors are naturally good at dealing with staff, "but many are small business people and so, like other business people, they can be penny-wise and pound-foolish."

As the medical practitioner, you are not generating revenue when you are not seeing patients. So a key to success is to get everything else in the practice to run smoothly without you, so you can focus on attending to patients. The practical way to do this is to appoint a chief administrator or office manager or CEO who runs the practice while you get to be "the doctor." An implication is that you need to find the right person to do this, and that a person with appropriate skills is extremely valuable.

Investing in a good administrator may be the most impactful use of your money. A good administrator should be able to manage all staff members (including hiring and firing), coordinate with suppliers, satisfy regulators, and set things right with unhappy patients. She should also have the skills to take the initiative in strategic planning, negotiating real estate leases and equipment purchases, as well as negotiating terms for financial agreements with insurers. In other words, the senior administrator is in charge of everything other than providing the medical services.

In recent decades, the importance of having a competent administrator has been recognized. Over time, the role has become more formalized with customized educational opportunities and credentials such as the Certified Medical Practice Executive (CMPE) credential offered by the Medical Group Management Association (MGMA). The MGMA describes itself as the "leading association for medical practice executives and leaders." Its mission is to advance the medical group management profession with a view to creating dynamic and successful medical practices that meet patient needs. In subsequent sections we will encounter the MGMA in several contexts.

Whether or not you directly supervise staff members, as the owner of the practice you need to hone your emotional intelligence and competence, including gaining an understanding of the people on your staff, what motivates them, and what alienates them.

Accordingly, this chapter proceeds with discussions of: key drivers of human behavior, classification of staff members as value creators, destroyers or spectators, as well as discussions of staff turnover, performance reviews, and retention.

Key Drivers of Human Behavior

Fundamental needs drive the behavior of all people. If you are having trouble attracting or retaining staff, look to these underlying Drivers for answers (listed in no particular order):

Compensation

Most people work to make a living. The hard currency they bring home is of utmost importance—it truly does put food on the table. People are happiest and most productive when they feel financially secure and their efforts are justly rewarded. Conversely, people resent being underpaid. The resentment will affect their motivation, morale, demeanor and longevity in the workplace.

Most people rely on a predictable paycheck when making important life decisions such as having a child or borrowing to buy a house, or car, or boat. Steadily setting money aside in children's college funds and committing money to retirement savings accounts also require predictable income.

Employers who cause "paycheck anxiety" (concern about not being paid) break trust with their employees. Once this fundamental trust is broken, loyalty erodes and staff are less willing to "go the extra mile." Under such circumstances your most talented employees are likely to be most disappointed, offended, or resentful, as they are likely giving up other legitimate opportunities to be with you. When the best people leave, a downward spiral is initiated: the practice performs even more poorly, causing more belt-tightening and further departures, and so on.

If paychecks are consistently late, incorrect, or employees believe they have been shortchanged, not only will you lose their services, you may find yourself having to respond to complaints filed with regulatory agencies.

Upward Mobility, Sense of Personal Direction and Satisfaction

Most people desire to advance in their careers. They take great pride in moving up the ranks, earning a greater share of responsibility in the practice, gaining their peers' respect, and reaping the financial rewards and personal satisfaction of advancement.

When that sense of direction or upward trajectory is in question, commitment wavers. The glass ceiling is an all-too-familiar assassin of motivation. Imagine the frustration of working hard, often for years—proving yourself every step of the way—only to be blocked by some invisible barrier. The longer the barrier is in place, the more likely employees will depart.

Surely, you say, glass ceilings and their equivalents are a thing of the past in enlightened medical practices. Isn't it the case that sometimes people don't get promoted because they don't deserve it?

Yes, that can be true, but too many managers adopt this explanation only to watch their best talent walk out the door. I'm not suggesting that you must promote people prematurely. I'm suggesting that you should recognize some obligation to develop individuals and to promote them to leadership roles when they are ready.

Here's an example. Several years ago I encountered a manager who expanded his medical consulting practice aggressively. His unit grew from 4 people to 19 in less than a year. By the end of that period, he had each and every one of these 19 people reporting to him directly. I asked him why he hadn't promoted a couple of them to intermediate leadership positions, with the more junior staff reporting to them in a pyramidal reporting structure. This would allow him to have fewer direct reports, making it easier for him to manage the organization. His answer was that none of them were worthy of a leadership position.

Over subsequent months the manager became (predictably) over-extended with people-management duties, and was unable to spend sufficient time with any of the employees. He was also unable to properly attend to all his other duties. Eventually, his staff deserted in large numbers. To this day I still find it impossible to believe that across that pool of talent, not a single person manifested sufficient skills to be rewarded and challenged with greater responsibility.

Clarity, Sense of Corporate Direction

People need to believe that the practice's long-term prospects are positive. They want and need a sense that management knows where it wants to go in terms of corporate strategy, and that it has the intellect and skills to achieve those plans.

Part of management's job is to share enough strategic thinking to satisfy employees that the corporate vision is clearly defined and achievable. If management does not satisfy this "(emotional) need/right to know," people will be more inclined to explore external opportunities.

Fun

People are much more likely to remain committed to an institution and continue to perform well when one very simple condition is met—they are having fun!

An enjoyable, stimulating environment is often at the top of an employee's list of job criteria; she may give up some financial compensation or upward mobility to maintain it.

Take away that fun, and the changes are sudden and dramatic. Why would anyone elect to give ground on compensation or mobility if they can't even enjoy their job? The answer is simple: the smart ones won't stick around.

When was the last time you heard "It just wasn't fun anymore!" as the impetus for leaving a position?

Personal Dignity and Respect

It's possible to be well paid, clear about the practice and its plans, and still feel victimized. If the practice treats a person as if his presence and contributions are unworthy, he's likely to be offended and consider leaving. Yes, immediate practical considerations or the lure of money may induce a person to stay for a time. But eventually the need for respect and appreciation will prevail.

One workplace infamous for significant pecuniary benefits but an abusive environment is Wall Street. Wave after wave of young and ambitious university graduates are fed into the Wall Street machine, where they spend as many years as they can stand working horribly long hours, subjected to a hostile and, at times, racist and sexist atmosphere. The average tenure in years may be counted on the fingers of just one hand. Employees toil until they come to the realization that their dignity is worth more than the paycheck beguiling them to stay in an emotionally (and sometimes physically) unhealthy setting.

One of the most common mistakes made by medical practice owners is to assume that throwing money at people will solve all problems. Throwing more money at a person who feels disrespected only fuels resentment. It may get the person to agree to hang around a bit longer, but it is not an effective long-term solution.

Sense of Control

Numerous studies show that all humans have an inherent need for a sense of control. Indecision, agitation and anxiety are common among people who have little or no say in what work they do, or when, where, how, or with whom they must share the work environment.

The longer people feel helpless, the greater their frustration and desperation to regain some control. If those efforts are not successful, they are far more likely to exercise their last option—to walk out the door and never look back. If their concerns stem from abusive management practices that violate the law, they may initiate lawsuits.

Predicting how a given individual will react to dysfunction is difficult. Some people may be willing to give up one or more of these elemental Drivers as a short-term sacrifice; but in the long-term, their fundamental yearning for fair compensation, promotion, direction, fun, dignity and control will win out.

Sometimes people do compromise, usually from necessity. Fun and compensation are the most commonly surrendered, not because these are unimportant, but more because people come to believe that expecting anything better in a dysfunctional situation is unreasonable. Each person has his own emotional "pain threshold"; once it is crossed, he'll begin to perform poorly and/or eventually decide to escape.

When people believe their leaders are committed to them and their well being, they will respond by voluntarily agreeing to compromise on one, perhaps more, of these drivers, provided that the sacrifice is well understood, and it's clearly finite. Dignity and respect are never negotiable, never to be sacrificed.

Value Creators, Destroyers, & Spectators

As you assess your staff (and your own actions), keep in mind that there are effectively 3 types of employees: (1) those who create or add value, (2) those who destroy value, and (3) those who are mere spectators.

Value Creators

Value creators are those who contribute positively to the firm's growth and well-being. They do their job well, pull their weight, innovate, collaborate, are emotionally competent and productive, and fit in socially with their peers. Value creators represent a good return on investment for the practice, and it's important to hire them, empower them, and keep them happy.

Value Destroyers

Value-destroyers are those who undermine others' efforts, waste resources, and/or behave dishonestly. They stifle others' creativity and enthusiasm, complain endlessly, cause delays, produce flawed work and generally undermine the practice's efforts (consciously or subconsciously). Value destroyers are a drain on the practice's resources, holding everyone else back. To improve the practice, these people must be reformed or let go.

Spectators

Spectators are those who take up space but don't add any discernible value. They may not destroy value but they are also not helping to move the practice forward. If you want your practice to be dynamic and constantly improving, spectators are not people you should have around.

In some cases, it's easy to identify value-destroyers, but the most insidious ones are not easy to pin down. Some trouble-making types you will likely encounter are:

The *Prima Donna*: The *Prima Donna* destroys value by demanding attention and resources.

The Eternal Pessimist and Morale Depressor: The eternal pessimist always sees the cup half-empty and his consistently dark attitude depresses the morale of others around him, affecting their productivity.

The Liar or Cheater: The liar or cheater chronically distorts the truth, creating confusion and frustration among colleagues, and/or engages in illegal behavior which may include theft or fraud.

Distinguishing the creators from the destroyers is important in any firm. A practice in a competitive environment can't afford inefficiency. It can't afford to carry people who not only do not contribute, but actually cause damage by taking up resources, producing inferior-quality products and services and having conflicts with colleagues.

In order to distinguish a creator from destroyer, ask yourself the following questions:

- Do his projects end successfully or unsuccessfully?
- Does he pull his weight or let others do the work?
- Do others resist or resent working with him?
- Do those reporting to him appear to be poorly-trained and resist having him as a mentor?
- Do his direct reports fail to successfully move on to higher responsibilities?
- Can any of his successes be attributed to other people?
- When volunteers are needed for a project, does he hide or raise his hand?

Be cautious when you suspect a value destroyer is acting illegally. Consult with an attorney to ensure your intended remedy is within the law.

Staff Turnover

One of the biggest issues in the services industry is staff turnover, which can be costly. Your practice must expend money when hiring: crafting, approving and posting ads, selecting candidates, interviewing finalists, and training new employees. The cost is even higher if you have to undertake some of these steps personally.

If you notice a pattern of high turnover at your practice, you must ask yourself why this is happening. Is there a middle manager who is scaring people off? Is *your* behavior or attitude contributing?

Seek to interview departing staff members in order to understand the real reasons behind decisions to leave. Often, people will be more open once they have decided to leave as they no longer need to fear retaliation in the event their criticisms are resented by management or colleagues.

If there is something festering within your practice, it's crucial to identify it as soon as possible. If you suspect that a middle manager is the cause of a staff member's departure, make sure that middle manager is not in charge of the exit interview. It may be a good use of your time to handle that interview yourself so you can sense what the real issues are.

Weigh all feedback carefully and seek to validate the information provided. You don't want to jump to conclusions and retaliate against a manager or employee who is simply the subject of vindictive comments, but you do need to know the truth.

Performance Reviews

Employees deserve to periodically receive performance reviews in order to fully inform them of what they are doing well and where improvements may be needed. Inexperience leads many managers to deliver less-than-honest performance reviews. Such reviews are most often systematically biased to the positive end of the spectrum. Some reasons include:

- A desire to avoid confrontation. This is a natural tendency, but a manager must have a backbone, and she can't shy away from managerial responsibilities. Delivering an honest review need not be a confrontational event. When a manager is consistently honest with an employee and holds ongoing performance discussions (not just one session at year-end), there should be no surprise, no shock, and no confrontation.
- A lack of certainty about what the employee has done over the review period, often due to lack of managerial attention. This should never happen. If a role (or job) exists, there is an implication that the role is valuable, and if that is the case, then that person deserves to be observed and to receive performance feedback. A manager must pay continual attention to her people and their development. She can't make up for a year of neglect in one day or one week.
- Failure to maintain personal distance from the employee. There's nothing wrong with becoming friendly with employees, but ideally managers should remain emotionally unattached, precisely so that when the time comes, they will be able to be perfectly (and even brutally) honest. It's easier to avoid getting too close than to have to reverse that intimacy at a later date.

- A concern the employee, who fills a critical role, may leave if the feedback is too harsh. This is a very common concern, but a manager can't be held hostage to what she thinks any single employee may, or may not, do. It's tempting to believe that certain people are indispensable, but history clearly shows everyone is dispensable (and this includes you). If there's reason to believe that a person in a critical role may depart, contingency plans should be set up to lower the firm's dependence on him well in advance of performance reviews. Even when the stellar employee is well loved and appreciated by all, the practice has a responsibility (that is, *you* have the responsibility as owner) to come up with contingency plans. For example, what would you do if the star employee suffered serious illness or injury? You must have some plans in place for *the day after*. Doing this in advance for all key personnel reduces your reliance on them and the leverage they have over you. A simple solution is to cross-train multiple employees so they can do each other's jobs if necessary.

Providing inflated positive feedback may seem easier in the short-term, but in the longer-term, it hurts the staff and the practice. The dishonest feedback deprives employees of an opportunity to identify deficiencies and work on improving their skills. This, in turn, means they won't improve in areas most critical to the practice. This means the practice won't be progressing and developing as it should. Furthermore, the staff will find themselves in an even worse state when they do finally encounter a manager (in the same practice or elsewhere) who provides honest assessments.

There is often an assumption that employees won't notice that little effort has been made in the review process, or that the feedback provided to them is insincere. In fact, people quite easily sense when their review is insincere or viewed as low priority. This leads them to question the commitment being made by the employer to their development, and ultimately to erosion of trust and loyalty. Conversely, people can tell when a sincere effort has been made to provide meaningful feedback. Even in those cases where the feedback includes some (constructive) criticism, the honesty is appreciated and respected.

Staff Retention

Eventually, all managers learn that the key to minimizing human resources issues is to identify good people and keep them happy. When good people are happy, the practice is an efficient and fun place to work and grow. Over time, as long as you are paying attention and using your emotional intelligence skills, it should become clear which employees are the stars to be retained and which ones should be replaced.

To secure the loyalty and services of the stars, you have a variety of options, which draw on much of the material we've already covered. Begin by recognizing and responding to the key drivers of human behavior:

1. Compensate fairly
2. Provide opportunities for advancement and satisfaction
3. Offer clarity and a sense of corporate direction
4. Nurture a fun work atmosphere
5. Treat everyone respectfully
6. Provide a sense of control

A fair approach to compensation may involve the use of benchmarking data to gain an understanding of what constitutes a fair salary per region and specialty. The Medical Group Management Association (MGMA) provides useful compensation benchmarks for physicians, complementing its mission of creating skilled medical practice leaders.

You can use a variety of benefits to attract and retain good employees. Medical, dental, vision, life and disability insurance, etc., can be very effective in making staff members feel appreciated and valued. (As noted earlier, a reliable and smoothly-operating payroll system is also a must. The experienced administrator along with your accountant will be able to direct you to providers of payroll systems).

An attractive benefits package may include:

- Health/Dental/Vision plan(s)
- Disability insurance
- Life insurance
- Vacation allowance

- Retirement plan contributions
- Pension plan
- Deferred compensation
- Profit sharing

Offering some or all of these benefits may seem expensive in the short-run, but can turn out to be good investments if they help to retain star performers—and avoid expenses and headaches associated with high staff turnover.

As noted earlier, while people like to be paid well, they are even more interested in feeling respected and valued. Jeffrey Ring and Sanford Fisher, owners of Fisher Ring CPAs, point out that it doesn't take much effort to send a signal to staff members that they are appreciated and valued. Taylor Shoffner, Director of Operations at Edward Lazer DDS Cosmetic & Advanced Dentistry, adds that successful practices provide their key employees with flexibility. She cites an example of a dental practice that hired an 18-year old as a chairside dental assistant. Noting her clinical skills as well as ability and interest in learning, they took the time to train and educate her. Over a 22-year period (and counting), they allowed her to work flexibly during her pregnancies, and nurtured her to the position of head administrator.

A successful practice must also treat its young medical practitioners well. After all, these may be the people to whom you'll want to sell your practice. Nurturing them helps build value in your practice, and equipping them with professional medical and business skills will enable them to pay you well for the business upon your retirement: a win-win for all concerned. Despite this logic, one occasionally comes across senior doctors who are reluctant to mentor junior members of the firm in anything that is not related to medicine. That is, there is a reluctance to share leadership and management wisdom. There can be various reasons for this which include (consciously or subconsciously) a reluctance to: (1) "waste" time on nonmedical issues, or (2) prepare potential future competitors in the event the young doctors leave and set up a competing practice.

As a medical group grows, it's important to hire young doctors who share the existing partners' values and priorities. Another word for this is culture. You've founded a practice with a particular set of values in mind, and it's wise to find others who believe in the same principles. This extends from how patients and staff members are treated, to how they are mentored, nurtured, and compensated.

Here's an example of a medical practice consisting of 6 physicians of the same generation with shared values and medical philosophy. At some point they decided some new blood would be a good idea, so they hired three young physicians. It soon became painfully clear that the older and younger cohorts embraced very different approaches to healthcare. The older crowd preferred to see a smaller number of patients and spend more time with each. The younger cohort preferred to see a larger volume of patients, with shorter patient-physician sessions. The resulting tension caused the entire practice to disband, harming all the physicians involved and their patients.

Financial Management

By all accounts (from physicians and dentists, as well as their accountants and attorneys) financial management is the most challenging aspect of owning a medical business. This isn't because finance is rocket science—it isn't. Rather, it's because medical practitioners don't normally receive sufficient exposure to finance concepts during their school years. Furthermore, many doctors find finance (and accounting) to be unintuitive and inaccessible. The latter is partly attributable to the fact that, much like medicine, finance has its own language.

In this chapter we discuss three crucial financial management concepts: (1) cash flow, (2) medical billing/coding/collecting and (3) financial statements. While financial management includes various other concepts, these three basic ones are likely to be of most immediate relevance to you.

Cash Flow is King

What is Cash Flow and why is it so important?

Cash flow refers to inflows (revenues) and outflows (expenses) of money. When all cash outflows are subtracted from all inflows, we get a sense of the net cash generated by a business over a specific period of time, for example, a year.

Unlike some accounting entries (such as depreciation or goodwill), cash flow in our context refers to real or actual cash. That is, the amount of money generated and available to make actual payments to creditors such as suppliers and landlords, as well as salary payments to staff members. Thus, cash flow represents the lifeblood of the business. Any missteps that leave you short of cash can be fatal, and hence, you must keep a close eye on cash coming in and going out.

A key observation is that having *expectations* of cash inflows in the future is not the same as having that cash on hand, and expected *future* cash flows won't help much if you run out of cash in the near term. So even though you may have high hopes for solid revenue inflows in three months' time, your business still has to survive over those three months. You still have to pay your staff, and suppliers, and landlord, and bank.

Miss one payment and you could find yourself in trouble. Labor laws require you to pay your staff in timely fashion; suppliers may cease to extend credit to you or may halt shipment of supplies; the landlord may begin legal proceedings against you; the bank may threaten foreclosure if you fail to make payments on your loans. Any one of these outcomes in isolation is really bad (but they usually come in bunches). This creates distractions, meaning less time for you to treat patients and therefore less revenue (exacerbating the cash flow problems even further and leading to a downward spiral). It also leads to dissatisfaction among the staff who may elect to leave just when you most crucially need them to help drive revenue. And it raises concerns for patients (who may wonder why there is an eviction notice on your door).

All start up businesses have cash flow issues. This results from the need for significant up front expenditures: to pay lawyers and accountants and suppliers and staff members—all before you have generated a single cent of revenue.

The remedy is careful planning. A competent accountant will help you to estimate your anticipated expenditures. You should complement this with a realistic (that is, not overly optimistic) estimate of revenues. The timing of these expected revenues is crucial. Don't fool yourself into assuming that money will immediately pour in. The forecasted shortfall between expenditures and revenues should provide a guide as to how much cash you will need on hand to meet expected expenditures. Add to this some amount to cover unexpected expenditures, and then strike a deal with your lender to extend that much credit to you in cash, or at least in the form of a revolving line of credit. And don't squander that money. Be highly disciplined and protective of your cash. It's the only thing between you and a painful and embarrassing bankruptcy.

Medical Billing & Collecting

In an earlier section I stated that a good billing system is the *lifeline* of your business. This is not an exaggeration. You can do everything else well, but dropping the ball on billing and collecting has the potential to destroy your practice. I also recently referred to cash flow as the *lifeblood* of the business. The complete analogy is that the billing and collecting tools are the vascular system—lifeline—of your business, while the material that flows through that system is the cash—the lifeblood. Carrying that analogy forward, if you want your cash flows to be properly contained and to reach their desired destinations (whether you are paying others or receiving cash from them) it is imperative that your business have a healthy vascular system or the infrastructure to track, deliver and receive cash.

In order to bill (insurers) properly for your services you must provide the correct codes that represent each distinct service or procedure rendered to a patient. The coding system has steadily become more complex over time. This has made it imperative that you (or more commonly your skilled colleague(s)) handle coding with care and precision. Mess up with private insurers and they'll put every barrier in your way to receiving payment (they do this even if you don't screw up, but when you make a mistake it gives them an excuse to drag their heels on payments). Any delay in processing your reimbursements means a delay in the arrival of your revenues. Meanwhile, your expenses still come due, leading to a cash flow problem.

When you make an error billing a private insurer your "punishment" is usually a delay in reimbursement. When you make an error billing a government entity, the outcome could be far more severe, especially if you are a repeat offender. For example, you could completely lose your access to this source of income.

If your business is heavily dependent on government reimbursement (e.g., Medicaid or Medicare), losing such access could be devastating. If you are suspected of fraud, your reputation, license(s) and entire career could be in jeopardy.

Melissa Pitchford, CFO of Katzen Eye Group and the President of the Maryland MGMA points out that fears of getting into trouble lead some doctors to "undercode", that is, code for less expensive procedures instead of more expensive ones—even when the more expensive procedure was performed. For the doctor's practice, undercoding means lower earnings. The correct approach is to bill correctly—not under or over code, and to support those codes with appropriate documentation.

According to accountants, billing is the number one gripe for physicians. Tellingly, it is rarely mentioned by dentists. This is primarily because most physician practices are highly reliant on agreements with the main healthcare companies (Blue Cross, United Healthcare, etc). The dental industry is different. It's much more common to bill clients directly, and it's the clients who have to chase the insurers for reimbursement. This means the dentist has more time to see patients and generate revenue, while the physician may instead find herself on the phone arguing with the insurance company.

It's relatively easier to collect from professional payors (for example, Medicare) and harder and takes longer to collect from individual patients. When it comes to individual patients, it's much more effective to engage them in a conversation regarding financial matters while they are in the office. The probability of successful collecting declines significantly once patients leave your office without addressing the issue. But many practices are too busy to ensure that such conversations take place before the patient exits.

Many doctors are at a loss when their billing is rejected or ignored. Instead of putting resources into collecting those unpaid bills, they simply shrug their shoulders, and move on. In doing so, many fail to recognize that they have just written off some of their practice's lifeblood. A patient who is desperately in need of blood can't afford to walk away from even the smallest amount that may be available.

Ms. Pitchford points out that medical practices are likely to have a contractual obligation to collect payments. That is, they're not allowed to shrug their shoulders and give up on those bills. Her advice is unequivocal: "Chase down the dollars you are owed or go out of business."

Many doctors hire a billing company to communicate with insurers, but the biller's staff may not be specialized enough. They may focus on the low hanging fruit. That is, those bills that are easiest to collect, while ignoring others. Some billing companies instruct their staff to spend X amount of time on a given case and then move on to others, even if the original case has not been resolved.

There are remedies available for a practice with subpar billing. Physician-turned-entrepreneur Jeffrey Hausfeld develops assisted living facilities, consults to health care companies and is a co-founder of the Society of Physician Entrepreneurs. Among other activities, he founded a debt recovery company, and shared the following example: Examination of a prospective client's records established that millions of dollars were uncollected. The firm's existing collection agency was doing next to nothing, and the practice's billing staff were filing away unfilled insurance claims that should have been pursued. After hearing this, the owners fired the existing billing staff. Within a few months the new service recovered $50,000 and about $200,000 of old insurance claims were reprocessed.

Getting a good billing system in place requires a combination of software and a competent billing specialist. Billing specialists must be knowledgeable and tenacious. They require ongoing continuing education as rules and regulations constantly change, and they must be fully up to speed to defeat insurers' latest roadblocks.

Why do insurers put up roadblocks? Insurers are often publicly traded companies. Such companies have a fiduciary or legal obligation to their shareholders to maximize profitability. Every day that a payment to a physician is delayed, means one more day having that money in the insurer's corporate bank account where it is earning interest (profit) for the insurer.

A remedy is to maintain immaculate records. Proper documentation of everything that goes on in your practice is crucial to resolving issues with insurers, suppliers, staff members, regulators, and unhappy clients. It is also one line of defense against internal fraud or embezzlement by staff. So be organized and diligent in tracking all information and making it available in timely fashion. Part of the solution, as noted above, is to have a competent person in charge of billing.

If you are outsourcing billing to a third party, you need to have a competent attorney review the contractual arrangement and convince yourself that the biller is going to add value.

Here's an example of what can go wrong, courtesy of attorney Wayne Zell. You contact the Billing company which sends you a standard form contract. The contract specifies a variety of conditions which apply upon termination of the agreement. You decide to review the document yourself and skim over it. Assured by the biller that it reflects standard language, you sign and return the agreement, then rush off to attend to a patient. Since this is the biller's standard contract, the termination provisions are likely written in favor of the biller. At some later point you decide to terminate the association with the biller, only to discover that you have some unexpected liability, due to the small print in the contract. Instead of a smooth transition to a more competent billing company, you are now required to pay tens of thousands of dollars to be released from the agreement.

Needless to say, asking an attorney for help *after* you've signed the document is going to be far more costly than having the lawyer involved upfront.

Alternative Service Models

High inflation in the cost of health care services has led to experimentation with various service models. The Affordable Care Act emphasizes a model known as *capitation,* in which medical practices receive from an insurer a fixed dollar amount per patient per year. The medical service provider must then run itself efficiently such that it provides all contractually-determined services under capitation's budgetary constraints. Under this model, the medical practice is incentivized to perform only necessary procedures and tests, thereby keeping costs under control. A criticism of this approach is that it may force providers to water down the quality of their services.

The prevalent incumbent model is *fee-for-service,* in which the medical practice is reimbursed for each individual procedure performed. This model is very common but has been criticized on the grounds that it rewards unnecessary procedures and medical tests, thereby creating skewed incentives that contribute to inflation in the costs of health care.

Think carefully about which model you wish to embrace for your practice, and hire people who are comfortable with that approach.

Financial Statement Basics

I can feel you rolling your eyes in anticipation of a scintillating discussion of accounting. To thwart the onset of boredom, perhaps this motivation will help: if you could manage your business more efficiently and retire 3-5 years earlier than planned, would you be interested?

Financial statements provide information on your practice's financial health and its performance. They can be used to tell you how well you are doing compared to prior years (performance analysis), how well you are doing compared to other similar practices (benchmarking), and even to estimate what you believe your performance will be in future (forecasting). The analysis can be at a very high (or general) level, for example, how much profit or loss has the practice generated over the last year? Or it can be undertaken at a more focused level to understand why performance is lagging. For example, are my support staff costs higher than average and are they causing low profitability? The point is that having detailed financial statements allows you to understand and manage your practice better.

Here's the medical analogy: In the same way that a doctor relies on measurements of vital signs (temperature, blood pressure, heart rate) to determine a patient's health and identify ailments, a manager uses financial indicators to highlight the weaknesses (and strengths) of a business.

Failure to understand and monitor your business can lead to the worst case outcome—bankruptcy. A far more common (but still unfortunate) outcome is that the practice is less profitable than it could be. This means less money to retain good staff, buy better equipment, secure a more favorable location, pay off corporate and student loans, and save for retirement. Seemingly small adjustments can pay significant dividends for your financial success, so it is well worth it to identify and remedy them. But you can't identify and make those adjustments if you are failing to measure and analyze.

We will focus here on two basic financial statements:

1. The Balance Sheet – a snapshot of the practice's state of financial affairs at a specific *point* in time (usually at the *end* of a

year or quarter). This includes quantification of assets, liabilities, and net worth of the business.

2. The Income Statement – a measure of income, expenses, and profit over a particular *span* of time (typically a month or a year).

The Balance Sheet

The main panels of the balance sheet are Assets, Liabilities, and Shareholder or Owner's Equity. These are always related according to:

$$Assets = Liabilities + Owner's\ Equity$$

Alternatively, this can be rewritten as:

$$Owner's\ Equity = Assets - Liabilities$$

Your owner's equity (how much the practice is worth now) is the difference between what the practice owns (the assets) and what it owes (the liabilities).

If you are seeking to become a part owner of a business, you may be expected to *buy-in* (purchase) some fraction of the firm's Equity. This will typically entitle you to a share of the profits corresponding to your percentage ownership. You will likely be expected to shoulder a proportionate share of the firm's liabilities (for example, loans outstanding to the bank).

It's normal practice to divide Assets into Current Assets and Long-Term Assets and similarly to divide Liabilities into Current and Long-Term. Current (or Short-Term) refers to items which mature or are due up to a year in the future, while Long-Term refers to any asset or liability with a maturity or due date greater than a year. Figure 2 reflects a very simple situation in which Furniture and Equipment is the only long-term asset and bank loans are the only long-term liability. Balance sheets can be much more detailed than the version shown in Figure 2.

Figure 2: ABC MEDICAL ASSOCIATES
Balance Sheet on July 1, 20XX

ASSETS

CURRENT ASSETS
Cash	$	90,000	
Accounts receivable	$	163,000	
Inventories	$	10,000	
TOTAL CURRENT ASSETS			$ 263,000

Furniture and Equipment	$	575,000	
TOTAL LONG-TERM ASSETS			$ 575,000

TOTAL ASSETS			**$ 838,000**

LIABILITIES

CURRENT LIABILITIES
Accounts Payable	$	125,000	
Accrued expenses	$	43,000	
TOTAL CURRENT LIABILITIES			$ 168,000

Long-term debt (bank loans)	$	397,000	
TOTAL LONG-TERM LIABILITIES			$ 397,000

TOTAL LIABILITIES			**$ 565,000**

OWNERS' EQUITY			**$ 273,000**

TOTAL LIABILITIES plus OWNERS' EQUITY (must equal **TOTAL ASSETS**)			**$ 838,000**

For financial management purposes, you can focus on individual numbers, for example, examine whether Owners' Equity has increased (by comparing last year's and this year's balance sheets). You can also create ratios and use those to analyze the firm's financial state.

Dividing Total Liabilities by Total Assets yields a *Leverage Ratio*,

Leverage Ratio = Total Liabilities / Total Assets
$$= 565,000 \: / \: 838,000$$
$$= 0.67$$

The Leverage Ratio reflects the extent to which the firm is indebted. A high number reflects a high level of debt compared to assets. This is generally unfavorable as the firm must make interest payments on all liabilities. Having a lot of liabilities or obligations means the firm has a high interest payment burden which reduces the amount of money available for all other needs, including salaries, bonuses, equipment repairs, etc. Failure to meet outstanding financial obligations in timely fashion can drive the firm into bankruptcy.

Another important ratio is the *Current Ratio*, a measure of short-term *liquidity* (how readily the firm can meet short-term financial obligations):

Current Ratio = Current Assets / Current Liabilities
$$= 263,000 \: / \: 168,000$$
$$= 1.56$$

Typical values for Current Ratio are in the 1.00 to 2.00 range. A higher ratio is better than a lower one, as it suggests the firm has more money available on short notice to service each dollar of liabilities. Being at or above 2.00 is usually quite healthy, although there are exceptions.

The Income Statement

The income statement (shown in Figure 3) contains two major sections: a listing of all sources of income (Revenue), and a listing of all expenditures (Expenses). The difference between these two represents the Net Profit (or loss) over a particular period of time.

You can examine the actual dollar numbers, or you can convert all entries into percentages of total income (revenue). This process is known as *common sizing*. (Balance Sheet items can also be common-sized—simply divide all entries by Total Assets). Common sizing allows you to compare the relative income and expense items of your practice to other practices. For example, you may identify that your support staff costs (salary and benefits) comprise 15.44% of total revenue while the typical practice in your field shows that these numbers are usually closer to 10.5%. (Before you panic, please note that I just made these numbers up for the purpose of this discussion). Ask your AA Team members for sources of appropriate benchmarking data for your particular specialty and geographic location.

Staff salaries and benefits tend to represent the largest expenditures for a medical practice, and it is therefore crucial to manage them carefully. The more detail you capture regarding staff-related expenditures, the deeper you can dig for answers and the more control you have in making changes and examining their effectiveness. (This example assumes a practice with two doctors).

Figure 3: ABC MEDICAL ASSOCIATES
Income Statement, January 1 - December 31, 20XX

	Amounts	% of Revenue
REVENUES		
Doctor revenues/Collections	$ 1,650,000	92.57%
Non-doctor revenue	$ 103,000	5.78%
Other income	$ 29,500	1.65%
TOTAL REVENUE	**$ 1,782,500**	**100.00%**
EXPENSES		
Doctor salaries	$ 560,000	31.42%
Doctor benefits	$ 85,000	4.77%
Total doctor salaries & benefits	**$ 645,000**	**36.19%**

Administrative staff salaries	$ 92,000	5.16%
Administrative staff benefits	$ 12,300	0.69%
Clinical staff salaries	$ 149,000	8.36%
Clinical staff benefits	$ 22,000	1.23%
Total non-doctor salaries & benefits	**$ 275,300**	**15.44%**
Billing service	$ 24,000	1.35%
Business insurance	$ 8,910	0.50%
Malpractice insurance	$ 28,520	1.60%
Dues, subscriptions	$ 7,130	0.40%
Furniture	$ 12,478	0.70%
Office equipment	$ 97,000	5.44%
Laboratory fees	$ 23,173	1.30%
Radiology costs	$ 70,473	3.95%
External professional fees	$ 19,608	1.10%
Marketing and promotion	$ 53,475	3.00%
Drug Supplies	$ 46,345	2.60%
Medical and surgical supplies	$ 87,343	4.90%
Administrative supplies	$ 32,085	1.80%
Other office expenses	$ 26,738	1.50%
Information technology	$ 17,825	1.00%
Telephones	$ 10,695	0.60%
Rent	$ 142,600	8.00%
Utilities	$ 71,300	4.00%
Miscellaneous expenses	$ 17,825	1.00%
TOTAL OPERATING EXPENSES (excluding doctor *and* staff costs)	**$ 797,523**	**44.74%**
TOTAL NON-DOCTOR OPERATING EXPENSES	**$ 1,072,823**	**60.19%**
TOTAL EXPENSES	**$ 1,717,823**	**96.37%**
GROSS PROFIT (EBIT)	**$ 64,678**	**3.63%**
Gross profit per doctor (2 doctors)	$ 32,339	
INTEREST EXPENSE	$ 35,650	2.00%
TAXES (assumed 25%)	$ 16,169	0.91%
NET PROFIT (after interest and tax)	**$ 12,858**	**0.72%**

Some basic ratios are:

Overhead Ratio = Non-doctor Operating Expenses / Practice Revenues
$$= \$1,072,823 / \$1,782,500$$
$$= 0.60 \text{ or } 60\%$$

The *Overhead Ratio* is designed to capture the cost of supporting those who generate the income in the practice. This is why the doctor expenses are excluded from the numerator, while Total Non-doctor Salaries and Benefits expenses (support staff) are included. That is: $\$1,072,823 = \$797,523 + \$275,300$

The *Accounts Receivable Ratio* is also important:

Accounts Receivable Ratio = Total Outstanding Accounts Receivable / Total Practice Revenue
$$= \$163,000 / \$1,782,500$$
$$= .0914 \text{ or } 9.14\%$$

Note that the Accounts Receivable number comes from the balance sheet while Practice Revenue comes from the income statement. This ratio estimates the fraction of annual income that is tied up in outstanding receivables (payments expected from patients or insurers but not yet received). A high ratio value means a lot of money is tied up (not yet received). In contrast, a low number reflects a favorable level of efficiency in collecting outstanding fees from patients.

It's also important to know how comfortably the practice is able to meet its interest obligations. This is especially crucial for a practice carrying high levels of debt. The *Interest Coverage Ratio* helps to give a sense of this:

Interest Coverage Ratio = EBIT / Interest Expense
$$= \$64,678 / \$35,650$$
$$= 1.81$$

EBIT is a measure of Gross Profit and stands for *Earnings before Interest and Taxes.*

There are many other ratios you can (and probably should) generate. More detailed analysis of financial statements is beyond the scope of this book. In consultation with your specialized accountant you should maintain detailed financial statements and formulate and track the various ratios that are most important to your practice. The American College of Surgeons or other medical societies may offer basic accounting courses in the event you feel a need for a deeper level of education.

Medical practices usually don't default (go bankrupt) because doctors are bad at medicine, but rather because doctors are bad at business. Even if your practice is surviving, it may not be as efficient as it could or should be. This means everyone works more hours, is more fatigued, has less time for family, experiences more acrimony in the workplace, and the practice is at greater risk of lawsuits by patients or staff. For all these reasons it is crucially important that you run your practice as efficiently as possible—and this means being a capable manager who understands the financial condition of your practice.

Know Your Revenues, Expenses, and Profitability

Here's an example of the kind of enlightenment your financial statements can provide, followed by action: Suppose you look at your business and want to increase revenues and improve profitability. Examining your financial statements you note that you are seeing on average 9 patients a day, while the benchmark for your specialty (obtained from your AA Team or external sources) is 16 patients a day. Meanwhile, your expenses are similar to benchmark levels. Eureka! You now realize that the underlying issue has to do with not seeing enough patients as opposed to being an issue of inflated expenses. You can now pay closer attention to the question: *why am I only seeing 9 patients a day?* Potential answers are: *my marketing is not effective; I spend more time per patient than the benchmark; my administrators are inefficient; I need one more examination room so I can host and examine more patients simultaneously. Perhaps I only looked at the summer months during which many people are on holiday. Instead, I should generate numbers for a longer period and revisit the issue—perhaps there is something about my expenses that is playing a role after all?*

Once you identify the underlying cause of the low profitability you can do something about it: improve marketing; spend less time per client (if possible without reducing quality of care); retrain existing administrator or hire new one; move to a larger location with more examination rooms, or rearrange the existing space to create an additional examination room.

In short, getting deep into your financial numbers helps to identify "where-the-rubber-hits-the-road" questions *and* to formulate meaningful answers. It also helps you to make a solid case to prospective lenders because you can prove that you are in control.

The good news, of course, is that you don't need to re-invent the wheel in coming up with answers to these questions. There are many medical practice consultants who will be only too happy to assist. These consultants provide a broad range of advisory services, including some of the most important needs specific to medical practices: billing systems, collections services, coding conventions, human resource management, regulatory compliance, HIPAA issues, and marketing services. Some medical practice consultants are highly specialized, so find one whose expertise is most relevant to your needs. A simple Internet search should yield some choices in your geographic area. Resources may be available through your state medical or dental society, as well as through national organizations. Your AA Team should also be aware of some good local candidates, and some accounting practices provide their own management consulting services.

Keep in mind that in the absence of detailed financial statements, you have no way to analyze your revenues, expenses, or profitability. Here's a sobering "know your revenues" example to close up this section. This is the story of a sole practitioner—a surgeon who did a lot of Medicaid work. He was known in his community as very gracious and generous to his patients. He did not maintain accurate financial records. As Medicaid began to steadily reduce payments, his revenues steadily decreased. His costs remained the same (and in some cases increased). The doctor had to work harder and harder just to maintain the same standard of living. The pressure led to depression and ultimately suicide.

It would be presumptuous to claim a full understanding of this physician's specific circumstances and state of mind. Nevertheless, the trend of declining reimbursements was apparent to many physicians. Those who knew the source of their revenues (and expenses) were able to proactively adjust and continue to make ends meet, successfully avoiding a tragic outcome. Because he did not have appropriate records, he was unable to make needed changes. By understanding your revenues (and expenses), you can act proactively to maintain a profitable and manageable business.

Fixed and Variable Costs

To effectively manage your practice you need to understand the distinction between two types of expenses: *fixed* and *variable* costs, and specifically how they impact your practice's bottom line or profitability.

Fixed Cost: A cost that does not depend on the number of patients seen or the amount of services provided. Monthly lease or rent payments are common examples of fixed costs. If your practice's monthly rent payment is $11,833 (or $142,600 annually), you are obligated to make that payment regardless of whether you see 10 or 100 patients in a given month.

Variable Cost: A cost that varies depending on the number of patients seen or the amount of services provided. The antiseptic treatment used to clean a room after each patient is an example of a variable cost. If you see 100 patients in a given month, you will have to use 100 antiseptic treatments. If you only see ten patients, you will only use 10 treatments.

Here's why these distinctions are relevant. The more patients you have, the more you can spread your *fixed* costs around. In the examples above, if you see 10 patients a month, the payment received from each of them effectively has to cover $11,833/10 = $1,183 of your fixed monthly rent payment. If you see 100 patients, each of them only needs to contribute $11,833/100 = $118 to cover rent.

An early-stage medical practice is usually not fully booked with patients, but it still has to meet its fixed cost obligations. That's why getting your patient count to at least cover those fixed costs is so crucial. Variable costs, meanwhile, remain low when you are seeing few patients. (Of course, ultimately, you do need the fees paid by patients to cover all your costs).

Another observation is that once your total revenues or collections from patients cover your fixed costs, each subsequent patient you see is more profitable, because the contribution to profit from that additional patient is only subject to variable costs.

An implication is that once your fixed costs are covered, you have more flexibility to reduce prices (perhaps temporarily) as part of a marketing campaign to bring in more prospective patients.

Each practice has its own tipping point, or threshold level of patients, at which fixed costs are fully covered. You need to keep this in mind as that tipping point signals a higher potential level of profitability.

Another financial management guideline is to use your assets as intensely as possible. For example, you are already paying rent. Using your facility more allows you to generate more revenue which can be used to cover costs and flow to the bottom line (as profit). You can achieve this by being open for longer hours, or by renting your facility to someone else (as long as this is permitted by the terms of your lease and does not breach client confidentiality). So, for example, you could rent your space out to a specialized medical group that wants to be open on weekends. Keep in mind that if the facility is open more hours, some variable costs will increase, for example, utilities (electricity and water).

If you have some specialized equipment that isn't easy to obtain, you could rent out time to other professionals on your machine. This is a way to use that tool more intensely. Again, your maintenance costs may increase as well as the costs of inputs to making the machine work (electricity, ink, paper, etc.), and these should be taken into account when deciding how and whether to pursue such income enhancement alternatives.

Planning for Retirement

Financial management of your business should also address your retirement planning needs. Ben Gorton, a retirement planning specialist with Retirement Planners & Administrators, Inc., points out that as a sole practitioner, you can contribute up to $52,000 annually into a defined contribution plan such as a 401(k). (You can contribute up to $57,500 if you are over 50 years of age). If you are an employee of a practice with multiple workers, you can make a salary deferral of up to $17,500 ($23,000 if over age 50) to such a plan, while the employer (the practice) may be able to contribute an amount that gives you a combined total of $52,000 ($57,500).

Regarding employer contributions, your firm should work with a professional to determine the correct amounts. The practice (employer) can deduct the contributions it makes to your plan, thereby reducing its corporate tax liability. You (as employee) are able to deduct your personal contributions (technically these are *salary deferrals*), lowering your personal tax burden in the tax year of the contribution. Investments in defined contribution plans grow tax-deferred, and you don't pay taxes until you begin to make withdrawals.

If you wish to contribute more than $52,000 annually to retirement planning vehicles, and to get tax deduction and tax deferral advantages, you can add a defined benefit plan on top of the defined contribution plan. Some of the key characteristics of defined benefit plans are that the practice must make contributions on your behalf for at least five years, and the contributions must be roughly the same size. That is, you can't contribute $200,000 in year 1, then zero in year 2, and $75,000 in year 3. Therefore, you must come up with an annual contribution amount that is manageable on an annual basis for the practice. Discuss this with your accountant and retirement plan specialist.

If as a self-employed individual you have both a 401(k) and a defined benefit plan, and in a given year you don't have enough to fund both, you can elect not to fund the 401(k), which is voluntary, and instead to fully fund the defined benefit plan obligation.

There are rules governing how much one can contribute to defined benefit plans. If you are self-employed, the limits depend on your age and your compensation level. In 2014, a 60 year old self-employed individual with plan-year compensation of $260,000 can contribute up to $236,382 to a Defined Benefit or Cash Balance plan. Of course, her practice would have to be sufficiently and consistently profitable to allow this level of contribution over at least five years.

If you decide to offer a 401(k) plan to yourself as an employee of your practice, you may have a legal obligation to provide some minimal contribution level to other employees of the practice. Consult with your retirement plan expert and attorney.

In addition to defined benefit and defined contribution plans, a corporation with employees can also set up non-qualified plan alternatives. Contributions into such plans may be deductible by the corporation, reducing its taxes, and funds in such accounts can often grow tax-deferred. Employees cannot, however, deduct such contributions from their personal taxes. Consult with your advisor about different types of non-qualified plans that can be offered by corporations.

Legal & Regulatory Considerations

We begin this section with a cautionary tale about a sixty year-old dentist who took on a new associate—a young dentist in his thirties. The younger dentist provided a contract documenting the nature of their working relationship. One day, out of the blue, the senior dentist received a letter from the junior dentist, which specified the older dentist's retirement date—two weeks away! Deeply offended, the senior dentist protested, pointing out that he intended to work for at least another five years. The junior dentist then referred to a clause in the contract, empowering him to force out the older gentleman. The moral of the story—get someone competent to read contracts before you sign them.

The observation that it's wise to seek a legal opinion invariably forces us to address the love-hate relationship that characterizes many doctor-attorney interactions. Let's begin with two factual observations:

1. The best way to protect your business and yourself is by ensuring that your contracts with suppliers, staff, partners, patients, etc., are comprehensive and well-worded
2. In the health care universe, laws are constantly changing

Combined, these two observations imply that you must seek and accept advice from a competent attorney.

If your feelings about lawyers are similar to those of your peers (many of whom were interviewed for this book), they likely include suspicion and resentment.

It may be informative to know the lawyers' perspective. Based on numerous interviews, that perspective is "life is too short to work with doctors." The bottom line is that many lawyers believe that:

1. Doctors don't like lawyers
2. Doctors "think they know everything"
3. Doctors don't like to pay money (especially to lawyers)

Whether or not we agree with these characterizations, attitudes on both sides reflect counter-productive distrust.

Logic dictates that given all the challenges faced by doctors, the last thing they need is to alienate the very professionals who can help them. Another way of putting this is with the reminder that the United States is ruled by law. As such, it is crucially important to understand the law and abide by it. Like it or not, lawyers understand this system. Most other people don't. Failure to obtain advice from a legal professional is almost always a bad idea. Trying to "self-lawyer" by reading about an area of the law online and writing one's own legal documents is dangerous.

Legal Contracting

Seasoned medical practitioners who own their own practices consistently acknowledge that as young physicians they were naïve about contracting. Here is an example: One doctor who owned a practice had another doctor working for him. The terms of the employment contract allowed the employee to work outside the practice. This seemed a reasonable allowance, enabling the employee to earn more money from external sources. But at some point, the owner realized that the employee was encouraging existing and prospective clients of the practice to be seen outside the practice, and he was receiving payments from them instead of the practice receiving those revenues.

The remedy in this particular circumstance, as explained by an attorney, is to specify in writing what kind of work employees are permitted to engage in outside the practice and what is allowed when dealing with the practice's patients or prospects.

The moral of the story is similar to this chapter's first example: as a medical practitioner you know a lot about medicine or dentistry, but not everything there is to know about contracting. Let the professionals (attorneys) take care of the contracts.

When you are considering getting advice on a document, ask yourself what is the worst case scenario if that contract is challenged. What do you stand to lose? How large would your liability be? The bigger the danger to your pocket book or viability of your business, the more important it is that you create an iron-clad contract with the help of a professional. Keep in mind that the more money is at stake, the greater the scrutiny of legal documentation by the counterparty. In response, you (through a qualified attorney) must protect yourself by engaging in the same level of diligence

Business Continuity & Exit Planning

Contract areas that are often neglected include business continuity and exit planning. *Business Continuity* refers to plans for maintaining the business in the event of a disruption such as the death or disability of a key partner (More generally, business continuity plans also address disruptions due to natural disasters or other factors). *Exit Planning* refers to mechanisms allowing a partner or owner to depart the firm in an organized manner. It may also refer to an outright sale of the entire business. In some cases, continuity and exit plans are both needed simultaneously. For example, when the key partner is disabled and a mechanism is needed to transfer her equity share to remaining partners.

In many cases, small practices don't have plans (and contracts) in place to deal with continuity and exit. This can be very dangerous for the practice, as well as the families of the partners.

Consider the following scenarios based on the assumption that you have formed a practice with two other partners:

1. One partner subsequently becomes disabled and can no longer participate. You can't fire the partner for two reasons: (1) you don't have the legal power to "fire" a partner and (2) his family relies on his income to survive

2. Alternatively, suppose that one partner dies rather than becoming disabled. His spouse is not a medical practitioner and is therefore by law not allowed to own a medical practice. Or, she is a medical practitioner but has no interest in working in your partnership. Or, you happen to find her extremely tiresome and annoying and wouldn't want her as a partner

You can proactively address these scenarios by drafting a *Buy-Sell Agreement* signed by all partners. Such an agreement should be created when the practice is first set up, and with the assistance of a qualified attorney. The buy-sell agreement explicitly lays out exactly what happens to a deceased or disabled partner's ownership stake under all potential scenarios. These scenarios include: disability, death, as well as what happens when a partner simply wants out.

In such agreements, death and disability scenarios can be addressed by having the business buy life and disability insurance, respectively, on each of the partners. In the case of disability, the affected partner receives a lump sum (or stream of payments) from the insurer while that partner's equity is returned to the business or distributed directly among the remaining partners. In the case of death the life insurance proceeds are provided to the deceased's family in exchange for the equity in the business, which reverts back to the remaining owners.

A different mechanism can be used in the event a partner wishes to be bought out. The buy-sell agreement can include a method for calculating the value of the practice at any point in time as well as a process for making payments to the retiring partner in order to buy out her share. It may be easier to provide the retiring partner a stream of payments over time, but if the firm can afford it, it may be possible to settle the matter by making one large lump-sum payment.

With the baby boomer generation retiring in large numbers, many older doctors are seeking to sell their practices. One of their laments is that few young doctors are interested in a long-term arrangement in which they work together for several years and then strike a deal in which the younger doctor buys the practice from the older doctor.

This has led many older doctors to adopt a simple but financially surprising exit plan: to close the practice down and retire. While this may seem to be the simplest solution, it means walking away from a lot of value. A list of happy clients represents a significant income stream—for which other doctors may be happy to pay good money.

Another consideration is that the older (retiring) doctor may have some potential legal (malpractice) liability. Instead of walking away from the business, it may be advisable to transfer legal responsibility for patients through a formal sale, or at least to use the proceeds of the sale to purchase Tail Insurance, discussed earlier in the Professional Malpractice Insurance section.

Regulatory Filings

Medical practices are subject to numerous regulations. To establish their abidance by these rules they are required to submit filings to various government agencies.

The penalties for failure to submit proper regulatory filings can be severe, including banishment from participation in programs such as Medicare/Medicaid, and even losing one's license to practice. Any of these penalties can be devastating to your business.

The implication is that you must be aware of your regulatory obligations, and you must complete them properly and on time. To do so, you need to have a competent administrator, and a reliable system to capture relevant information for filing and/or to respond to audits.

A resource for regulatory compliance may be found on the Practice Management section of the American College of Physicians® site, at www.acponline.org.

Credential Management

The credentials of all staff within your practice will be closely scrutinized by payors (insurers), regulators, and patients' attorneys in the event a legal claim is considered against you. If you seek affiliation with a hospital, your credentials will be scrutinized yet again by the hospital. In all cases, you and/or your practice will be examined and evaluated based on legal and professional ability to meet client needs.

Michael Simmons, CEO of CredSimple, strongly suggests you ensure that your practice properly tracks the credentials of all professionals. This applies primarily to your doctors but also to allied health professionals (nurse practitioners, physician assistants, registered nurses, dental assistants, etc.). Everyone must be properly licensed to practice in your state, and must complete all continuing medical education (or other) requirements in advance of deadlines.

One credential-related constraint (and especially for those private practices providing services under agreements with insurers) is that new doctors sometimes must "sit on the sidelines" for several months while their credentials are being verified. This can create a cash flow problem for the practice, which may be obligated to pay a new doctor for several months before that doctor is fully credentialed to bill for her time.

Keep this potential constraint in mind as you contemplate bringing new medical professionals on board. More generally, plan ahead and ensure you identify and abide by all credentialing requirements.

If all payments to your practice are from private sources, for example, in the case of elective plastic surgery or cosmetic dentistry, the credential management process may be simpler, consisting primarily of establishing that everyone involved has a proper license to practice in the State.

Best Practices

This chapter addresses some key practice management issues you are likely to face. The emphasis is on identifying and embracing best practices.

There is a very large body of knowledge to be mastered in achieving best practices. Not only are you required to stay current on the latest medical procedures, you also have to be on the forefront of regulatory compliance and business practices. That's a lot to keep up with, and generally more than any one human can or should handle.

In this chapter we will focus on business practices. Pursuit of medical procedure and regulatory compliance best practices is well beyond the scope of this business book, so I'll restrict my comments to reminders that you remain connected to the latest discoveries, medical procedures, and compliance requirements through reading of appropriate journal articles and completion of continuing medical education. In some cases you may prefer to have colleagues (other doctors) stay on the cutting edge of the science while you focus more on business issues. That is fine, as long as someone within the practice is bringing in the new ideas and developments that will keep your practice medically competitive. Similarly, you'll need someone within the practice to stay on top of the latest regulatory requirements.

Your local medical or dental society can be a good source of information on best practices, including considerations that are specific to your region.

While we cannot possibly address all business best practices in this volume, we will address some of the most important ones, including: installing a capable head administrator, reinvesting in the business, determining your ideal practice size, setting priorities and expectations, acting decisively, adopting a constructive mindset to billing and coding ("the Paging Dr. Goldilocks" section), pre-empting negative dynamics among owners, and tapping into the collective knowledge of professional groups or collectives.

Install a Head Administrator

The first best practice is to divide the workload. In most cases the logical separation is for you—the doctor—to lead the provision of medical services, while a head administrator takes care of everything else. In earlier chapters I referred to some key employees (in particular administrators) as being worth their weight in gold. They are valuable precisely because they can take over management of various responsibilities, allowing you to focus on what you do best—providing outstanding medical services to patients.

The practice earns its highest income when you are billing for your services. To maximize revenue, put yourself in position to earn as much as possible by seeing as many patients as you can. Every minute that you are distracted by other activities is a minute that is lost to you for potential revenue generation.

The right administrator can make your life a lot easier, and your practice more productive. She can take care of human resource management issues, billing and coding, ordering of supplies, compliance, coordinating with the landlord, etc.

Increasingly, with medical services becoming more competitive and sensitive to regulatory issues, a properly qualified administrator is a must for any practice seeking to perform professionally. The Medical Group Management Association (MGMA) offers a certification program that strives to equip its members with many of the skills listed herein (by way of the Certified Medical Practice Executive (CMPE) credential). Qualifying examinations and essays, as well as a sequence of continuing education requirements are designed to ensure that graduates of the program remain in touch with regulatory changes and innovations.

Kathy Maddock, Vice Chair of MGMA's Eastern States section, and a senior administrator at the University of Maryland School of Medicine, points out that access to best practices is a compelling reason to join state or national organizations such as the MGMA. In the absence of such connectivity, many small medical practices can become isolated. For example, in some small practices the office manager is a person with informal credentials and relatively few professional connections. Instead, it can be more advantageous for the practice if the office manager is connected to a friendly, collaborative organization that provides structured education and easy access to constantly evolving best practices.

While you can hand off oversight of various functions to an administrator, as the firm's owner you still retain ultimate responsibility for the practice's successes and failures. Accordingly, you must satisfy yourself that everything within your practice meets your high standards and is consistent with your values.

Reinvest in the Business

To introduce this subject, here's an example of a physician who had some personal financial issues and in response proceeded to strip his practice bare of all value. Squeezing the practice manifested in refusing to allow annual salary increases to staff, not paying bonuses, neglecting regular maintenance, and failing to update equipment and technology solutions. All this happened against a backdrop of tightening regulations. Eventually, wholesale changes became necessary to address new compliance issues. Because the doctor had failed to keep up, much larger expenditures and a deeper commitment from staff were needed to catch up. But because of the belt tightening the staff had become embittered, suspicious and unwilling to accept the additional headaches required in order to upgrade the practice. When the dust settled, the doctor was left with an empty shell instead of a vibrant practice. He had outdated systems, worn out old equipment, and no reliable staff members. Needless to say, the practice failed, throwing his barely repaired personal finances into disarray once again.

While a sole proprietor (or a group of partners) is well within his rights to pull earnings out of the practice, doing this to excess will harm the business. Embracing best practices includes re-investment in the practice and the people employed by the practice. To maintain vibrancy, replace ancient equipment and consider providing continuing education opportunities to your employees, including bringing in outside speakers to address recent business and medical innovations.

Determine Your Ideal Practice Size

In every business there is a tradeoff between having a larger practice with more resources, and the increased managerial distractions of managing a larger space and greater number of people. Think carefully about the size that's right for you. That is, the one that allows you to enjoy professional satisfaction, financial success, and appropriate time with family.

There is no cookie-cutter single ideal size for everyone, and of course, your specialty also influences the ideal size. For example, practices that require large capital investments in expensive, specialized equipment often need to be larger to spread out the fixed costs over a larger number of patients. While expanding your practice to take advantage of cost efficiencies may be a good idea, more employees and a broader menu of medical services also add complexity to your operations.

You can achieve efficiencies without necessarily ramping up your own operations and associated costs. One option is to ally with providers of complementary services. For example, a practice of general physicians can set up a referral sharing agreement with a nearby cardiology practice, or a general dentist can do something similar with a specialist such as a periodontist. In either case, the alliance increases your local footprint by giving your practice broader access to prospective patients.

Other alliances may include sharing of staff members. So instead of paying a nurse to work for your small practice full-time, you can share her time with a nearby practice. Both practices get the skilled help they need, and neither has to pay for a full-time employee.

Give a lot of thought to whether you want an *exclusive* alliance with another provider. If you are agreeing to share referrals with only one specialist, it may be reasonable to expect the same level of commitment from them. For example, it may be unfair if you refer all your patients to one specialist, but that specialist doesn't refer all her patients to you.

Strive for balanced agreements with counterparties of similar size and clout. An alliance with a much larger counterpart can mean you will be bullied. A partnership of equals is more stable and generally easier to manage.

Regardless of the type of arrangement you pursue, always give yourself the flexibility to reverse course or amend the agreement. That is, all contracts must allow you an "out" or exit clause. Otherwise, you may lock yourself into an unfavorable situation. A competent attorney can help to ensure you have ways to exit unfavorable arrangements. But keep in mind that the attorney should review the alliance agreement *before* you sign it!

You have the greatest amount of control when you stick with a small and manageable practice. But insisting on staying small can mean giving up good growth opportunities, and there are notable disadvantages to being small in today's highly regulated age. It can be difficult for small (and especially solo) practices as they must shoulder all the regulatory burdens on their own. This can be very expensive in terms of direct costs to purchase systems and hardware, and to train staff to use the systems. And you also face indirect costs which may be less obvious but can also significantly affect efficiency and profitability. Indirect costs include the distraction of the owner and other staff members whenever these systems require managerial attention. Finally, small practices are especially precarious because if anything happens to the owner/practitioner (death, disability), most of the value in the practice disappears. In contrast, larger and more balanced practices have professionals on hand who can cover for a missing colleague and maintain the value of the practice.

In light of the inherent disadvantages of being small in a highly regulated area, it can be tempting to chase growth, in particular through purchases of other practices. This often seems like a simple and easy way to achieve scale and greater marketing power. Business people refer to this tendency as *empire-building*, and it often results in a large and unmanageable business. There should always be solid business reasons for increasing a practice's size, and those reasons must be backed by concrete and objective numbers (revenue and cost forecasts).

Set Realistic Priorities and Expectations

Prioritize

Most likely, you won't have too much difficulty coming up with a "to do" list of action items for your practice: the problems will be to decide which items on the list to pursue first, second, third, and whether to revise the order when circumstances inevitably change. In any case, any preferences you have will likely be subject to resource or time constraints.

Begin by pursuing those actions that yield the greatest impact for the practice (usually in terms of lower costs and/or increased revenues). Success with these priorities will give you more breathing room to pursue others.

Priorities depend greatly on your planning horizon: if you are focused on surviving for one more financial quarter (3 months), you will likely make very different decisions than if you had the luxury of planning for a three-year horizon. The choice of horizon may be out of your control; it may depend on your banker insisting on a firm deadline for loan repayment, anticipated legislative changes, external macroeconomic factors, priorities of fellow owners, etc.

When you come across a process that is working, even if somewhat imperfectly, consider leaving it alone for the moment: the issue can always be revisited later, while in the near-term you can move on to other more pressing needs. Your (constantly evolving) Business Plan should reflect the decision to leave certain items or processes as they are, along with a statement of intent to return to these items when time and funding permit.

Set Expectations

Expectations are constantly being formed by staff, peers, patients, suppliers, etc., whether or not you are intending to create them. It's better to proactively shape expectations than to scramble for a response after disappointment has set in.

Mismanagement of expectations is one of the greatest failings of management, and may come about for several reasons:

- The manager is unaware his actions or inactions are creating particular expectations

- The manager is aware of the expectations that are being created but genuinely believes they are realistic, when in reality they are not
- The manager is aware that expectations are unrealistic, but is too concerned with the immediate repercussions of a public admission of financial troubles or scandal to admit the truth
- Occasionally, there is a hope (or a prayer) that in time, some significant event (a miracle) will arise, allowing the original expectations to be met

Unrealistic (inflated) expectations cause anxiety for all concerned. When compensation is tied to performance, the inability to meet unrealistic goals will quickly lead to disappointment and staff departures. Such defections make it even harder to meet the next set of corporate expectations, which can lead to a vicious circle, exacerbating the challenges facing the practice.

Act Decisively

Inefficient or outright dysfunctional practices often have indecisive leaders. We could engage in a philosophical discussion over which is the cause and which the effect (does indecision cause dysfunction or *vice versa*), but the bottom line is that once both indecision and dysfunction are present, they are mutually reinforcing. The only way to break this damaging cycle is for you, the leader, to begin to make decisions quickly and firmly.

Don't burden yourself with the notion that your decisions have to be perfect. No one makes perfect decisions. It's generally a good start to just make a few solid decisions relatively quickly. Military and corporate leaders agree it's better to make a decent decision quickly than to wait endlessly for the perfect plan to materialize. By the time you get to that perfect plan, the enemy or competitor will have overrun your position or your markets.

This apparent surrender to mediocrity is sometimes difficult for doctors to accept. They are trained to succeed, and less-than-perfect decisions can lead to severe complications for patients, including death. For people driven to success and perfection it can be difficult to accept what seems to be a band-aid solution. So they wait, sometimes procrastinating for weeks or months.

But there are times when applying a quick band-aid or its equivalent makes logical sense. For example, in an emergency room a patient is brought in with arterial bleeding from the leg and severe blood loss. The first priority must be to stem the bleeding, even if the effort is less than perfect. Once that immediate solution has been applied you can turn your attention to performing a more comprehensive examination to ensure you have identified all ailments. It doesn't do anyone much good to stop arterial bleeding in the leg, then walk away, only for the patient to die from a severe concussion and hemorrhage inside the skull. But logic dictates that you address the arterial bleeding, however imperfectly, to buy the time to deal with the other serious issues.

In a business setting you never have all the facts you want (often also the case in a medical setting). Therefore, you can't expect to make perfect decisions. But you should be decisive and move on to other priorities. The act of decisiveness is not just for you. Much of it is aimed at sending a signal to those around you (employees, patients, suppliers, etc.), that someone with confidence is in charge and that everything is okay.

Paging Dr. Goldilocks

This section primarily addresses the different mindsets or approaches owners apply to regulatory compliance, record keeping, and coding for billing purposes.

Dr. Under Radar

Dr. Radar strives to maintain a small practice; one that's so insignificant as to avoid attention by regulators. Dr Radar is certain that the practice is beyond scrutiny, and allows coding, collecting and regulatory compliance processes to get sloppy. When regulators do (inevitably) show up, the practice fails the audits.

Regulators have increasingly paid more attention to small practices, so there is no escaping their scrutiny.

Dr. Blissfully Ignorant

Dr. Ignorant fails to plan and by default embraces poor coding or collecting practices. The practice suffers from inefficiencies, steadily losing ground to competitors and becomes vulnerable. When trouble strikes or regulators step in, Dr. Ignorant has no idea what has happened, how to defend choices that have been made, or what to do in future.

Dr. Overly Conservative

Due to paranoia regarding regulatory oversight, Dr. Conservative always assumes the worst, and does everything to remain within the regulatory guidelines. While conservatism can be advisable, it's possible to go overboard, in ways that make the practice less competitive or efficient. For example, Dr. Conservative may under-code due to concerns that any higher codes (leading to higher fees payable to the practice) will raise eyebrows and criticism from payors. Dr. Conservative may also embrace overly onerous regulatory practices that lead to higher costs and greater distractions leaving less time for treating patients.

Dr. Too Aggressive

Dr. Aggressive concludes that raising revenue is easy, and instructs everyone to over-code. Payors and regulators are constantly on the lookout for precisely these abuses. When they step in and demand supporting paperwork, the practice is unable to provide such material. Repercussions can be severe, including fines, loss of license(s), and even jail terms.

Dr. Goldilocks

It should be clear that Drs. Radar, Ignorant, Conservative and Aggressive are all adopting sub-optimal mindsets, leading them to take on too much risk and/or to squander some of the potential returns or rewards. Instead of being overly conservative or too aggressive in your coding and collecting, be just right—be Dr. Goldilocks.

Begin with the assumption that at some point in time regulators will knock on your door and will audit your practice. Since you are now under the mindset that this will happen, the proper response is to be organized, have all systems set up properly, maintain appropriate records, etc.

Once you have all appropriate records, you will have all the data on hand to justify your coding and billing. You will put yourself in position to earn well, and to sleep better at night. Instead of having to live under the radar, you'll feel comfortable stretching your wings, as your practice's efficiency and transparency allow you to grow further.

Pre-empt Negative Owner Dynamics

Most medical practices are set up as partnerships. This means you must deal with partners who may hold different opinions about various strategic and tactical choices for the practice. One of the most common causes of medical practice dysfunction and failure is the inability of partners to work together constructively. Sole proprietors are not exempt from these considerations: they may at certain points of their career want to consider joining a larger practice, they may need to hire other doctors as employees on a part-time basis, or they may need to work with other medical practitioners when they seek to sell their practices.

According to Sage Growth's Don McDaniel, in cases of multi-doctor practices, each partner is often focused on maximizing his or her own income. "If a practice has three partners, the entity acts more like three independent businesses that share expenses rather than one cohesive business." This often results from partners not having any formal business training and a lack of awareness of the synergies or benefits of collaborating toward a common goal. Instead, each of them views the world from a very personal perspective. When they find they are making decent amounts of money, they ssume that all is well, not realizing that a more cohesive view of the artnership could lead to greater efficiency, better quality, faster nnovation and higher profits.

Most of these benefits come from taking advantage of economies f scale. As we've already noted multiple times, since the octors/partners should be focused on seeing patients, it's sensible to nd a professional manager or administrator who can identify fficiencies and suggest innovations. With a 'neutral' administrator in place, the partners can all turn their attention to doing what they do best—delivering high quality medical services to patients.

Physician-turned-entrepreneur Jeffrey Hausfeld provides the following scenario: Consider a practice with $1,000,000 in revenue. There is one administrator who is paid $50,000 annually, but is not very competent. A better administrator could improve efficiencies by at least 2% (and often a lot more). Improving efficiencies in the office by 2% means an extra $20,000 a year which can go to: hiring a much better administrator (at a $70,000 salary), improving the practice's premises, moving to a better location, improving the patient experience with one more part-time nurse, or enhancing the owner's retirement fund.

Business efficiency is hugely important, and doubly so if you have aspirations to expand a practice. Expanding an inefficient practice is likely to destroy it.

In most smaller medical partnerships that don't feel a head administrator is affordable, there is one doctor who is more interested in business and management, and ends up taking the lead on these matters. The other doctors, who are more interested in delivering services, are happy to let her do so. But this raises an issue—how should she be compensated? Should compensation be the same as that of those only practicing medicine? Should it be lower? Higher?

There is no set answer to such questions. The correct outcome depends on how much time is spent on each of the activities (medical versus managerial), and whether the doctor/manager does a good enough job to elevate the practice's performance.

Once the practice gets large enough it usually makes sense to hire a full time person who can take care of managerial issues. A doctor-turned-professional-manager could take the job, or it can be given to a head administrator. Larger practices (often those with more than fifty employees) are much more likely to employ a complete management team consisting of a Chief Executive Officer, Chief Operating Officer, and Chief Financial Officer.

Repeating earlier advice, the best way to avoid acrimony among partners due to misunderstandings is to document each partner's responsibilities, privileges, and compensation mechanism in writing. The same document should also account for changes over time in these obligations and privileges. The assistance of an experienced attorney is highly recommended.

Join a Professional Group

We've already noted that pursuing best practices is a big challenge, especially for small medical businesses with limited resources.

One way to overcome these disadvantages in a cost-effective manner is to join a professional practice group. Such groups may consist of one to two dozen local professionals, all of whom share an interest in networking, socializing, and learning from each other. Ideally, such groups contain a maximum of one member per medical specialty. This avoids competitive issues within the group and allows everyone to express their interests and needs more openly.

Groups may meet six to twelve times a year, often over lunch or dinner, and may be facilitated by a professional consultant.

Participation in a professional group can be an efficient and enjoyable way to learn and to improve one's practice, while meeting other talented and interesting people who can become peers, allies and friends.

As trust is built among group members, it's possible to explore joint marketing initiatives, sharing of staff costs, sharing of physical space, or sharing of equipment, all of which help to reduce overhead and increase efficiencies.

Groups are also useful forums for discussing and debating new medical ideas, approaches, legislation, technologies, suppliers, etc.

If you're interested in joining or forming such a group, please feel free to contact me through the Pillars of Wealth website (pillarsofwealth.com).

Be Proactive

The starting point for best practices is to be proactive. Instead of reacting to events in *ad hoc* fashion, in which you have to scramble for answers *after* the fact, try to anticipate challenges and have responses planned *in advance*.

Anticipating dangers and taking actions to mitigate them in advance is referred to as risk management. Given the importance of this topic it's addressed in greater detail in the next chapter.

Risk Management

We discussed personal or household risk management in Book I of this series, and applied some of that thinking to employment contracts. We now revisit this topic within the private practice context.

In this chapter we cover: a summary of some risk types you are likely to face in private practice, your first line of defense against risks (being proactive), the importance of periodically asking "what if", and preparing a Plan B.

Risk Types

Below is a list of some typical risk exposures for private medical practices, along with basic advice for mitigating them. At any time, your practice is likely to have exposure to most if not all of these dangers.

Operational Risk

All businesses face *operational risk*, which is the danger that the business will suffer losses due to human error, systems failure or fraud. Training and embracing good processes can help reduce human error. Well-tested systems (purchased from reputable vendors with good support infrastructure) can alleviate systems issues. Honest employees selected through a rigorous recruitment process and ongoing oversight by owners can minimize fraud.

Fraud risk is greatest when doctors blindly rely on others. Anecdotally, I estimate that a quarter of all doctors interviewed for the *Pillars of Wealth* series acknowledged having been defrauded by an employee—with losses ranging as high as $250,000.

The risk of fraud is the main reason why doctors must maintain some active oversight over administrators, who often have the most access and therefore greatest opportunity to commit shenanigans on a large scale. Doctors must know enough about the business to have a sense of cash flow and profitability. They must know which questions to ask when the numbers look odd. They must put in place internal controls that reduce the likelihood of fraud.

Fraud causes much more than financial loss. It also leads to a general erosion of trust within the practice, and a heightened sense of paranoia. Owners who have been victimized by fraud may never regain the confidence required to make fully objective decisions in future.

Credit Risk

For a medical practice, *credit risk* is the danger that creditors (for example, patients) will fail to pay money they owe the practice. Most medical practices suffer some losses from unpaid bills. When these amounts are negligible, it may be economically logical to ignore them and move on to higher priorities. But when the practice is strapped for cash, and/or the amounts owed are significant, such delinquencies can push the business into bankruptcy.

To alleviate this problem, the practice can vet payments more carefully, by not accepting personal checks or ensuring that credit card charges are successfully verified by card companies before a sale is finalized. Use of third party financing (discussed in Part I of this book) also ensures that the practice receives its money upfront. In these arrangements, the practice pays a fee (a fraction of the total bill) to the financing company, in exchange for transferring the credit risk to the financing company. If the client doesn't pay, it is the financing company (which has already advanced payment to the medical practice), which must chase down delinquent debtors.

Regulatory Risk

Regulatory risk refers to losses or penalties due to failure to meet regulatory compliance requirements. We've already discussed the dangers that arise when a practice is deemed to have breached rules or regulations. Breaches may include failing to maintain patient privacy or to abide by labor laws. Penalties may include fines and or loss of license. The remedy is to be well organized and educated regarding the latest regulations and compliance requirements. Regular (annual) reviews and a competent and experienced administrator or specialized consultant can help to perform such reviews.

Legislative Risk

Legislative risk is the risk that new laws will be introduced, negatively affecting your activities.

One example that comes to mind is that of the adult day health care industry in California in 2010. With the state government reeling from budget shortfalls, the governor of California attempted to cut funding to hundreds of adult day health care facilities, serving primarily elderly and disabled adults. A pitched legal battle ensued, and the industry eked out a partial victory that allowed it to survive under far stricter eligibility requirements and reduced reimbursements. Many centers went out of business. The move was a surprise for most, as many assumed the Democratic governor would work to preserve these services. But the financial pressures on the state were so severe that the unthinkable happened, threatening to derail services for tens of thousands of patients and put thousands out of work.

In addition to being aware of state-specific rulings, it's imperative that you fully understand the implications of the various federal health care acts and the political dynamics seeking to expand or repeal elements of these acts. Be aware of which political camp appears to be in the ascendancy as this has implications for the direction of future legislation which may impact you directly.

There are likely local, regional or national medical societies that share your concerns regarding certain pending legislation. Working in concert with these groups may allow you collectively to thwart or amend onerous legislation.

Legal Risk

Legal risk refers to potential for legal liability. The obvious examples are cases of legal action initiated by, or on behalf of, patients. Remedies include: (1) enhanced training to reduce instances that lead to lawsuits, (2) good communication between staff and patients to identify issues and deal with them constructively (some lawsuits can be avoided by diffusing a patient's anger or frustration proactively), (3) purchase of appropriate malpractice or other liability insurance.

Obsolescence Risk

Obsolescence risk refers to the risk of falling behind in technology and best practices, to the point that one's practice appears outdated to patients and partners.

An obvious example is a dental practice's need to embrace the latest solutions in pain management. Universally, people are concerned about the pain associated with dental treatments. Those practices that are able to allay such fears most effectively have a significant advantage. You must be aware of the latest innovations in this area and have the courage to experiment with some of them. By leading the change to a new treatment you can carve out a niche as modern, proactive, and committed to patient care. In contrast, dragging your feet on new technology will make your practice appear outdated and out of touch with patient priorities.

Similarly, web-based technology that makes appointment-setting easier, and other systems that increase efficiencies and reduce patient wait times have become increasingly important. As many practices embrace these innovations, those that fail to do so stand out more, in a negative way.

The industrial revolution in the 19th Century was characterized by mechanical engineering and machinery. It ushered in the age of assembly lines and automated manufacturing. The 20th Century was the century of electronics and information. Many believe the 21st Century will be about biology and biotechnology, with revolutionary advances in medical instrumentation and genome sequencing leading us ever deeper into living molecules and innovative medical treatments.

This sets the stage for a highly dynamic and competitive health care industry—your industry! More than ever before, it's imperative to be among the innovators rather than among the laggards or dinosaurs who refuse to acknowledge and participate in that inevitable change.

Leadership Risk:

Leadership risk refers to the dangers posed to the practice due to poor decision making by its leaders or owners. Common leadership errors include the absence of business continuity plans in the event an owner is disabled or otherwise unable to see patients and procrastination when various other decisions are needed.

Leadership risk can be mitigated by: (1) pursuing management knowledge to increase owners' expertise and reduce the likelihood of management errors, (2) hiring a competent administrator to provide management and leadership while medical professionals attend to patients, (3) remembering at all times that the "buck stops with the leader," and being willing to make decisions in timely fashion, and (4) accepting objective professional advice when it is needed.

This book assumes you are the owner or part owner of a practice. This means *you* are the potential source of the leadership risk. If you wish to succeed, you must minimize the danger you pose to the practice. This means being open minded, anticipating change, as well as being proactive, consistent and fair to those around you. The worst thing you can do is to be the firm's greatest liability.

High Financial Leverage

Leverage reflects the ratio of the firm's liabilities to its assets (how much it owes divided by how much it owns): the higher the indebtedness, the higher the firm's interest payments on debt, and the greater the strain on the firm's finances. Many businesses fail because of high leverage.

Cash flow volatility can lead to situations in which there is insufficient cash to cover interest owed. Technically, at this stage creditors can step in and initiate legal proceedings to shut the practice down and sell its assets off in order to recoup money they are owed: this ever-present threat often causes highly indebted (highly leveraged) firms to cut back on expenditures. These cutbacks may include slashing bonuses, eliminating perks, and foregoing otherwise needed investments in new equipment, technology or office improvements. The associated stress may also affect management's behavior, lowering staff morale and in turn, creating more anxiety.

The best way to avoid high leverage is not to take on high debt to begin with. One alternative is to start your operations on a small scale—i.e., a smaller office, with lower lease obligations, lower build-out costs, fewer employees, etc.—which means you can make do with smaller bank loans. After you successfully build a loyal patient base, you can make plans to expand.

Adverse Macroeconomic Factors

Adverse macroeconomic factors are ones that no single individual or company can control, such as unfavorable interest rates or energy prices. When interest rates go up, the increased cost of funding ongoing operations imposes strains on many firms. This is particularly the case if you have borrowed funds from a bank in the form of a variable rate loan or line of credit.

Higher interest rates may make it more expensive to finance new equipment purchases. They may also make it harder for patients to pay for elective services which are often financed through third party loans (for example, for cosmetic dentistry or surgery).

High interest rates, or alternatively high oil prices, generally depress economic activity by making services more expensive to provide (as your costs go up) and demand for services to decline as consumers (patients) feel the financial pinch.

Other commodities or inputs can also affect your practice. For example, if the price of a material used in medical supplies or equipment goes up (silver, copper), manufacturers of these items may raise prices, causing your costs to increase.

The answer to adverse macroeconomic factors is to be efficient and to react nimbly when the aforementioned forces begin to turn against you. Some examples: embrace energy efficient equipment to help mitigate spikes in energy costs; reduce debt in anticipation of rising interest rates; reduce staff hours in anticipation of slowed demand for your services.

Business Cycle

Economists often refer to the *business cycle*, which consists of a period of economic growth, ultimately reaching a peak, followed by a slowdown and subsequently a downturn, eventually reaching a trough, and then moving back up again. The phases within the business cycle are often correlated with macroeconomic factors such as oil prices, interest rates, unemployment rates, etc.

Depending on circumstances, a cycle may last anywhere from about five to twenty years. Unlike some of the other risk factors discussed in this chapter, over which you may have some control, you cannot stop business cycles from occurring. But you can prepare for them.

When a downturn occurs, there is typically a decline in demand, and a glut of supply due to excess capacity which had been built-up during the previous expansion. The excess capacity may come in the form of real estate for medical practices (due to too much construction in recent years), the number of practices offering services (and competing with you), extensive inventory of products, multiple equipment suppliers, advisors, etc. Downturns mean less money in patients' pockets, and tighter conditions for government reimbursement programs. All of these can mean downward pressure on your practice's earnings.

Be aware of the prevailing business cycle phase when opening for business or planning an expansion. Lower demand for your services during a recessionary period can present challenges, but it also provides some opportunity. For example, real estate prices and lease rates tend to be quite low during depressed economic periods. These can be the best times to (re)negotiate a lease or purchase a property—as long as you are comfortable that your business can generate sufficient cash flow to weather the downturn and then ride the subsequent economic improvement up.

One of your best defenses against business cycle movements is to run an efficient practice. All your competitors are going to be facing similar challenges, which means that the order of the day becomes *survival of the fittest*. You want to be among those who survive, and your best chance at achieving this is by being more efficient than others. Survival over a tough stretch provides significant rewards. When your weaker (less efficient) competitors go out of business, you can win over some of their clients. This means that you can come out of the recession in better shape than you entered it—but you have to run a tight ship *before* the recession hits!

It can also be wise to negotiate a generous line of credit with your bank *when times are good.* During such expansionary periods banks are all too happy to extend credit and usually at relatively low interest rates. The key is to not use that credit until it is really needed. Think of it as an emergency source of funds.

One of my friends opened a dental practice during a recessionary period. He began on a small scale, keeping costs low, took advantage of low lease rates, readily available used equipment (since many practices were shutting down and selling equipment), and had his pick of good employees because so many had lost their jobs elsewhere. As the economy picked up, he was well positioned to take advantage and grow the practice. Then his costs began to gradually increase: higher wages to retain good staff, lease renegotiations, and replacement of worn-out equipment. But the advantage was that by this point he had a successful practice, and an efficient and hardy one that had been "born" during tough times.

Competitive Landscape

Competitive landscape refers to current (and future) competition your practice faces. The competitive intensity your practice faces depends on your location, the number of existing rivals, the extent to which your area is already saturated by them, barriers to entry of additional competitors, and the potential appearance of new competitors leveraging innovative technologies or solutions that place you at a disadvantage.

It's imperative at all times to remember that there are others who are seeking to offer services similar to yours, and they will be all too happy to get their hands, drills, and scalpels on your existing and prospective patients.

Historically, competition in the medical practice space was limited to other local practices that catered to the same population as yours. Technological innovations now allow some doctors to communicate with patients and prospects through video screens, and specimens for lab tests can be picked up and delivered almost anywhere for analysis. The upshot is that others can infringe on your turf from another county, state, or even another country.

Consider the following example: electronic images of X-rays, CT scans, MRIs, etc., can now be cost effectively transmitted to other countries, where lower-cost physicians can examine them, write up reports, and transmit them back. This type of solution opens the door for physicians in countries with far lower labor costs to compete with doctors in the United States. Is it possible that some local radiology practices may decide to cut their local physician staff in half and utilize foreign doctors to perform some basic analyses?

The implication is that even traditionally sheltered medical activities may see their competitive position undermined by technological innovations. The conclusion is that you must be on the lookout for any and all competitive threats and make plans to meet those threats from a position of strength. That is to say, act proactively to be the one with the advantage and press that advantage home, rather than waiting passively for the day when competitors have overwhelmed you and taken your patients.

Once you fall behind, it's much harder to catch up to everyone else.

Geographic Over-Extension

Geographic over-extension refers to situations in which a business opens up multiple locations, thereby stretching itself too thin. While expansion can create access to new pools of prospective patients, the expansion can also lead to higher costs and may adversely affect your lifestyle.

The "tyranny of distance" includes higher logistical and overhead expenses such as transportation costs, expenses associated with mastering multiple regulatory regimes (in cases of multi-state expansion), the costs of additional office space and equipment, as well as communication challenges. These challenges may complicate knowledge transfer, strategic planning, and thwart efforts at providing consistent services in all locations.

Firms that cannot yet afford a critical mass of personnel in all distant offices may have to send scarce resources (experts) to provide local guidance and assistance. These frequent visits can prove very costly in financial terms, and may reduce the morale and productivity of over-extended, fatigued, home-sick travelers. One of these fatigued and demoralized experts could be you.

An example that comes to mind is that of a dentist with a successful practice who sought expansion. His current region was saturated so he ended up purchasing a practice in a community that was under-served. The two locations were 4 hours drive apart, and he committed to making this trip twice a week to kick-start the new practice. In his zeal to practice in an under-served area, he hadn't fully considered the physical toll of travelling such distances so frequently. His family was unhappy with his early morning and late-night arrivals. He was tired and edgy. Ultimately, he had to sell the second practice because he simply could not handle the distance. As a side note, he had attempted to find a local dentist who could run the practice for him, but the area was so remote that no candidates came forward.

Reputation Damage

Reputation risk refers to damage that results from your reputation (or that of the practice) being tarnished.

To realize long-term success a medical practice must honor the trust placed in it by patients, employees, suppliers, and regulators. Many firms can survive economic downturns, adverse regulations, as well as increased competition. But reputation damage can quickly prove fatal. When a firm stumbles morally (or when there is even just a perception that it has compromised its integrity) trust with all market participants is undermined. Competitors are sure to make the most of the opportunity by poaching patients, staff, and partners.

The advent of the Internet age has made reputation damage much more severe and prolonged. Any person with a grudge can post complaints (warranted or unwarranted) and leave a permanent smudge on your reputation.

One example is that of a cardiologist whose practice was the subject of several unfavorable online reviews on yelp—posted by staff members! The object of the criticism was the office manager, whom staff accused of verbally abusive behavior. The damaging posts continued to plague the practice long after remedial action had been taken against the office manager.

In today's information age, anyone at any time can publish an unfavorable review of your practice or of you personally. To mitigate such risks it is necessary to be professional, fair, and proactive. Many complaints can be addressed successfully before they appear online or in the office of a government agency. This can be achieved by recognizing their underlying causes early (whether among patients or employees) and taking steps to remediate them. Allowing the aggrieved party an opportunity to vent is usually a good idea, followed by an apology, and some soothing gesture such as a discounted service or whatever seems appropriate to bring closure.

Concentration of Suppliers or Referral Sources

Concentration risk occurs when you rely too heavily on just a handful of suppliers or patient referral sources. This is the proverbial "putting all (or most) eggs in one basket" situation.

Why are these considerations so crucial?

These issues are crucial because a medical practice that relies on one primary source of referrals or supplies is more susceptible to declines in revenue when that one concentrated source suddenly disappears. The disappearance can be the result of the referrer/supplier going out of business, striking a more lucrative agreement with other provider(s), or severing ties with you due to some perceived slight or reputational issue associated with your practice. The point is that your revenue will take a big hit if referrals dry up or if you are unable to provide services due to lack of supplies or equipment.

For these reasons, one of the first questions a corporation will ask when considering any corporate acquisition is "how concentrated is the target company's client base or supplier base?"

In response, always seek to diversify your sources of revenue and supplies.

The First Line of Defense

As noted earlier, the first line of defense is to be *proactive*. Anticipate risks and deal with them before they turn from a probability of something bad happening, to the certainty that something bad has happened.

Proactive steps may include:

1. Hiring qualified people and allowing them to do their job
2. Paying staff well to keep them motivated and aligned with the practice's long-term goals and aspirations, which include high customer and employee satisfaction
3. Making sure that new additions to the team share the values and culture of your practice
4. Investing in the practice (installing new systems that make the practice more efficient, protecting sensitive information, and improving client and staff experiences)
5. Investing in the owners/partners by giving them educational opportunities to improve their business, financial, leadership, and management skills
6. Diversifying patient referral sources
7. Having relationships with multiple suppliers of equipment and other necessary items for running your practice
8. Having a buy-sell agreement in place (described in an earlier chapter) in order to anticipate and address inevitable changes of ownership
9. Ensuring insurance coverage is up to date and in force
10. Having an emergency fund of cash on hand to cover surprises

A good reason for the latter is that occasionally reimbursements from government sources are delayed. Causes of delay may include government shutdowns or temporary cutbacks. As a small business owner there is nothing you can do to force a lumbering bureaucratic government agency to release your funds earlier. But you still have to meet payroll obligations, and pay your suppliers, and contribute to pension or retirement plans, etc. Having several months' worth of operating cash in an easily accessible repository protects you against such reimbursement delays.

Each of these proactive steps improves the practice's expertise, professionalism, or preparedness, and reduces the probability that things will go irreparably wrong.

Ask "What If"

Use your imagination to simulate future scenarios and play them out to a logical conclusion. Some typical scenarios include: *What would I do if my business partner dies or becomes disabled? What would I do if I had one large contract for referrals from a hospital and that source suddenly dried up? What would I do if regulatory costs increased beyond a certain dollar value per patient?*

Get your staff members together and challenge them with this or similar scenarios: Imagine coming into the office on a Monday morning to find out that a supply or equipment order is late. Repeated efforts to contact the supplier fail. It takes several days to determine that the supplier has gone out of business or is the subject of some legal or regulatory action. You can't afford to wait. You need to keep your practice alive. Do you know which alternative supplier to call? The answer turns out to be no. Instead you must scramble to find a last minute alternative, which will put you in a position where you may have to agree to unfavorable pricing and the concern that the new supplier may be no better than the previous one.

Anticipating dangers and gauging your level of preparedness is as simple as setting some time aside to ask the question "what if…" and playing that game through to unearth the related risk exposures.

Prepare a Plan B

Once you've asked "what if" and identified your practice's particular risk vulnerabilities, you should prepare a Plan B to thwart those vulnerabilities (in some cases you may even want a Plan C). The more likely a given negative scenario and the more devastating its potential outcome to your practice, the more detailed and refined a plan you should put in place.

Remember Ben Franklin's axiom: *failure to plan is planning to fail.*

Continuing the earlier example of your supplier disappearing, imagine if you had a Plan B. Instead of a desperate scramble, you or your administrator can calmly walk over to the filing cabinet, pull out the folder of alternative suppliers, make a single phone call, and settle back with the comfort of knowing your order will be filled properly and in timely fashion.

All responsible organizations are proactive, ask "what if" and prepare alternative plans. Emergency responders and hospital emergency units routinely follow these procedures and seek to improve best practices. There is no reason why you can't or shouldn't do the same.

Yes, resource constraints mean that you can't prepare for everything. But asking "what if" should help you identify and prepare for the potentially most devastating risks.

Words of Wisdom

One way to summarize the objective of this book is as follows: *to impart to doctors the collective wisdom gained by their peers.*

This chapter presents a compilation of pearls of wisdom drawn directly from comments by physicians, dentists, and other health care professionals, all of whom have learned private practice lessons the hard way.

In private practice you realize for the first time that you have no clue about finances, or about running a practice. You need to run a business AND manage student loans, a household, a young family, a new car, a home purchase and furnishings. Then you realize that you have no retirement saved up and nothing put away for children's college.

Doctors in private practice should at all times keep in mind the "George Steinbrenner effect" [reference to former New York Yankees owner]—just because you own the business doesn't mean you know how to manage the team and play all the positions all of the time.

Doctors often don't understand all the details and behind the scenes challenges of running a business. We are used to getting immediate responses from colleagues and nurses in hospital settings (where outcomes are life or death). We're unaccustomed to asking/demanding and not getting what we want or think we want or need.

It's important for doctors to learn to work in teams and negotiate (a lot of doctors are used to solitary studies and work). In the hierarchical world of medicine, there is rarely any negotiating. There is only ordering around of junior people. The idea that one must use skills to influence and negotiate is important for business success.

Doctors often underpay their administrator or office manager and nurses and other staff. The turnover can be very damaging in private practice. While in a hospital setting a doctor can be domineering and hospital human resources staff must find and hire replacements for departed employees, in private practice the owner must spend his/her own time finding, interviewing and training newcomers. It is best to repeat this process as little as possible. You are better off hiring good people, treating them well and paying them enough to make them happy. In the long run, your financials will be better than what you'd get from engaging in an ongoing cycle of firing/hiring and being forced into lower quality patient experiences due to manpower shortages.

Common mistake is to hire first candidate in the door, which only sets stage for more poor performance, firing, departures, etc. Take the time to find good people.

There's a lot of drama inside these [private] practices so need to learn to communicate with staff and treat them well.

Start small if possible and grow wisely.

One of the most dangerous moves you can make is to try to expand an inefficient practice—you will fail.

A big challenge for doctors is that their office manager acts as gatekeeper and may limit access to the doctor (for good or bad reasons). Bottom line is that this insulates the doctor/owner from what is going on in the business. In the worst case, the doctor has no control and becomes reliant on the administrator. This opens the door to embezzlement.

Objectively analyze any employment offers you receive. Don't be seduced by what you are shown when a practice is courting you. Look for the catch. There may not be one, but just in case, be skeptical enough to think clearly.
Never discuss finances directly with a patient. Patients' questions regarding money and insurance should be discussed with designated staff members—but never doctors. Failure to create this separation puts the doctor in a "greedy" light.

Patients often already think the doctor makes too much money ... Getting caught up in a debate about payment can only have negative consequences.

Some bosses in private practice are reluctant to share knowledge about practice management because they view such knowledge as having a competitive value. They fear that young doctors will take that knowledge and open a competing practice across the street. This hampers the younger doctors' ability to learn and grow as business people. Avoid being in such situations.

Doctors need to understand that business analysis is a science and a respectable one. Striving to be a good business person does not make you a "capitalist pig." It makes you a person who strives for good outcomes. Outcomes that allow you to provide more care to more patients, while minimizing risks that could place you or your practice in financial or legal danger.

Additional Words of Wisdom applicable to work-life balance may be found in Book I of this series.

Appendix 1: Purchase an Existing Practice

There are several paths to becoming the owner of a medical practice:

1. Building a new practice from the ground up
2. Working in someone else's practice and buying-out the original owner(s)
3. Buying a practice from a third party

Implicitly, we've assumed the first path in this book—the startup route.

When it comes to purchasing an existing practice (paths 2 and 3 from the list above), there are two potential approaches: a stock sale and an asset sale. As will be made clear below, the asset sale is the generally recommended path if you are the purchaser, while the stock sale approach has its appeal if you are a seller.

Purchasing a medical practice is a serious undertaking. The process is too complex to address fully in this book, so I limit my comments to several highlights, with a view to introducing you to some of the major challenges and dangers. You should engage the services of experts (in particular, a qualified and experienced attorney) and undertake appropriate due diligence.

Stock Sale

In a *Stock Sale*, you are buying the entity outright by purchasing 100% of its stock. You end up owning everything the legal entity owns: websites, furniture, inventory, equipment, existing contracts, etc. You also end up owning the firm's liabilities.

The seller generally gets to book all proceeds of the sale as long-term capital gains. From a tax perspective, this is far more favorable than proceeds being taxed at personal ordinary income tax rates.

According to attorney Michael Limsky, this tends to be a good deal for the seller, but not necessarily a great deal for the buyer. Why? During the sale process, the seller must make representations and warranties about the state of the assets and ongoing or anticipated liabilities, legal actions, audits, etc., faced by the firm. But even if speaking truthfully, the seller may be unaware of pending liabilities in the form of a lawsuit or an Internal Revenue Service (IRS) audit. As the buyer, you must protect yourself from such unknown liabilities, and the first line of defense is not to "buy" these liabilities in the first place. Instead, the buyer can seek to purchase the existing practice's assets (not the stock).

Asset Sale

In an *Asset Sale*, you buy assets of the existing practice—not the stock. This means you are not purchasing the underlying legal entity, which also means you should not be liable for that entity's legal liabilities (whether currently known or unknown).

The process is usually facilitated through creation of two lists. The first list comprises those assets you are explicitly buying. The second list specifies those items you are explicitly excluding—that is, *not* buying. It can be wise to include on the first list a statement saying that you are also buying other items that may not be listed explicitly. Creating these lists helps to reduce misunderstandings and potential recriminations at a later date.

With an Asset Sale, it's necessary to allocate the total purchase price to appropriate asset categories for tax purposes. Both sides must report the same allocation to the Internal Revenue Service, so you must reach agreement.

Asset categories typically include:

Furniture, fixtures and equipment (FFE) – these can either be written off immediately or over a few years by the buyer (potentially reducing the buyer's tax bill), so the buyer wants as much of the purchase price to be allocated to FFE. The seller, on the other hand, will likely have to recapture its depreciation expense to the extent the seller previously depreciated such assets, and then a capital gains treatment to the extent it may have had a gain on such property after the depreciation recapture. In plain English, the seller will likely have to pay taxes on the portion of the purchase price allocated to FFE.

Supplies – the inventory of supplies owned by the practice will also provide the buyer with an immediate expense deduction for the cost of the supplies. Seller will have ordinary income to the extent of this allocation which will be subject to tax.

Restrictive covenants (non-compete provisions) – this is a list of actions the seller is prohibited from taking. Some examples include: soliciting of clients in the practice that has just been sold, using confidential information, or starting a new practice within a certain distance of the one sold and within a certain period of time.

A portion of the purchase price will be allocated to the restrictive covenants (non-compete provisions). On the dollars allocated to this asset category, the buyer will have a 15 year straight line write off, and the seller will have ordinary income subject to tax.

Goodwill – this refers to assets whose value is intangible. A common example is reputation. The buyer must use straight line depreciation over 15 years for goodwill, which is not as favorable as other asset classifications. The buyer is better off trying to have assets classified as FFE. The seller, on the other hand, will typically treat this income as long-term capital gains income—which is taxed at a rate which has historically been lower than ordinary income tax rates.

Restrictive covenants are subject to state-specific interpretations. In some states, restrictive covenants may not be allowed at all. In other states the Court (that is, a judge) may be permitted to revise ("blue pencil") a covenant deemed to be overly restrictive to the seller; to reform it to fall within what is deemed permissible within that jurisdiction. In some states an entire restrictive covenant section could be nullified if it is deemed overly punitive. This could allow the seller to start a new practice across the hall from you and take all your clients away! Restrictive covenants are important for protecting your new practice for a period of time that allows your practice to take root and thrive, so pay attention to them. You want them to be as strong as possible, while avoiding the possibility that they may be struck down or amended by the Court system.

Transitions

You will also want to come to agreement regarding a variety of transitional issues, some of which are listed below:

1. How does one deal with patients who have work in progress? For example, dental patients who are halfway through their treatment plan? The buyer doesn't want to inherit half-completed cases. A solution is to give the seller access to the premises to finish up cases. It may be reasonable to charge the seller some agreed-upon amount of money for office expenses and supplies used.
2. What happens to accounts receivable from insurers, which may belong to the seller? You need to agree contractually on what is to be done with such funds, and how to identify them.
3. What about patient credit? Patients may be owed some money from the practice—do they maintain those credits with the buyer or the seller? On the one hand, as a buyer you may not want to have to honor credits provided by the seller. But you also don't want the clients to seek out the seller in his new location in order to use their credits (because they may then decide to join the seller's new practice instead of yours. It may be most sensible for you as buyer to honor the credits and attract those patients to your own practice.
4. What about reworks or *redos*? These are more common to dental practices, where a filling or cap must be reworked. Who is responsible for completing such work? As a general rule, you don't want to inherit any liability associated with such fixes, so it may be best to let the seller retain responsibility. You can give the seller access to the practice to deal with clients who have such issues.

The buyer should apply and/or register with all insurers accepted by the seller's practice. This is necessary to facilitate having your new practice's name on all checks received from insurers. Otherwise checks from insurers will continue to come in the seller's name.

Insurers may know you are about to buy a business because you've sent them your applications, but most will not process your applications and payments until you send them a final bill of sale. That can take as much as 30-60 days. Keep this in mind as you work on your timeline and cash flow estimates, and always remember that insurers have little incentive to make payments in timely fashion.

In the purchase/sale paperwork, you should include both the selling entity name (the business name of the practice) and the principals of the seller as parties to the agreement. That is, the names of individual medical practitioners who worked at the practice should be listed explicitly. Why?

According to attorney Michael Limsky, there are three reasons:

1. The buyer may want to use a principal's name in advertising, for example "this was formerly the practice of John Smith, DDS"

2. To ensure restrictive covenants apply to all the principals and not just their old legal entity. You don't want the principals to start a new company across the hall from you, and the way to do that is to specify that the restrictive covenants apply to them in addition to the old entity which is now an empty shell

3. To ensure *representations and warranties* (statements and assertions made by the counterparties in the contract) are as accurate as possible. Having the principals personally guarantee representations and warranties provides a strong incentive for honesty

In general, you'll want covenants, representations and warranties to survive the closing for as long as possible. One to three years may be typical. In some states having the contract signed under "seal" can extend the statute of limitations on representations and warranties.

Mistakes

Here's an example of a poorly thought-out purchase. The practice in question was owned by a highly skilled general dentist who was also able to provide some highly specialized and very profitable services. This made the practice more valuable. But that extra value could only be realized by a similarly skilled dentist. The purchaser didn't have the broader skill set and could not bring in sufficient revenue to support the loan used to buy the (expensive) practice. Within two years of the purchase being finalized, the business failed.

This was a transaction that should never have taken place. The practice should have been sold to a practitioner with the correct skill set to maximize revenue. The bank, which was new to the field and didn't pick up on the skills mismatch, was unable to gauge the buyer's deficiencies.

Another common mistake is that doctors rarely understand how much legal paperwork is required, and don't budget enough time for the process to play out.

Finally, an often neglected consideration is the need to lock in key staff members. Prior to closing any deal, you should be satisfied that: (1) you know who the key staff members are, and (2) they are comfortable with you being their new boss.

The Lender's Perspective

Before lending to you for the purpose of financing a purchase of an existing practice, a bank will want to see detailed equipment and furniture lists, the layout of the proposed practice, and a business plan. The bank will likely try to put liens on all those assets as collateral.

The bank will also want to closely examine restrictive covenants in the proposed contract. It is more likely to lend you money if it is convinced that you have in place some solid protections against competition.

A specialty lender may give you 100% financing plus some working capital if it is convinced you and your management team are capable and focused. It may agree to take the practice as collateral. But a non-specialty lender (or a somewhat skeptical specialty lender) is more likely to demand a spouse's signature on the loan or it may put a lien on your home. Needless to say, you want to avoid providing personal guarantees which may place your personal assets at risk. The bank may also prefer to direct you to a Small Business Administration (SBA) loan. An SBA loan may require a guarantee fee and you may have to cover extra costs for an SBA attorney.

References and Additional Resources

The American College of Healthcare Executives (ACHE) is an international professional society of "healthcare executives who lead hospitals, healthcare systems and other healthcare organizations." ACHE offers the Fellow of the American College of Healthcare Executives (FACHE®) credential. http://www.ache.org

The American College of Physicians enhances "the quality and effectiveness of health care by fostering excellence and professionalism in the practice of medicine." http://www.acponline.org

The American Dental Association (ADA) "is the professional association of dentists that fosters the success of a diverse membership and advances the oral health of the public." http://www.ada.org

The American Dental Education Association's (ADEA) mission is "to lead individuals and institutions of the dental education community to address contemporary issues influencing education, research and the delivery of oral health care for the health of the public." http://www.adea.org/

The American Medical Association (AMA) promotes "the art and science of medicine and the betterment of public health." http://www.ama-assn.org

The Association of American Medical Colleges (AAMC) represents all accredited U.S. and Canadian medical schools, as well as hundreds of teaching hospitals, health systems, and scientific societies. http://www.aamc.org

Bar-Or, Yuval. *Pillars of Wealth: Personal Finance Essentials for Medical Professionals*. Ellicott City: TLB Publishing, 2014.

Goleman, Daniel. *Emotional Intelligence: Why It Can Matter More Than IQ*. New York: Bantam, 2005.

Jena, Anupam B., Seth Seabury, Darius Lakdawalla, and Amitabh Chandra. "Malpractice Risk According to Physician Specialty." *New England Journal of Medicine* 365.7 (2011): 629-636.

The Medical Group Management Association (MGMA) is an association for medical practice executives and leaders. It provides "the networking, education, advocacy, tools and resources to build strong practices." The MGMA offers the Certified Medical Practice Executive (CMPE) credential. http://www.mgma.com

The National Association of Physician Recruiters (NAPR) "is dedicated to the enhancement of all physician recruiting activities through a spirit of openness and cooperation in the exchange of ideas and the pooling of resources." http://www.napr.org/